# Build YOUR Space

## HOW TO CREATE AN ACCESSIBLE HOME THAT IS PERFECT FOR YOU, YOUR FAMILY AND YOUR FUTURE

## Julie Sawchuk

Sawchuk Accessible Solutions

Blyth, Ontario

Sawchuk Accessible Solutions

Blyth, Ontario N0M 1H0

www.juliesawchuk.ca

Book Layout ©2017 BookDesignTemplates.com

Ordering Information: Go to www.juliesawchuk.ca or order on Amazon.com or Amazon.ca

Quantity sales. Special discounts are available on quantity purchases by corporations, associations, and others. For details, contact the "Special Sales Department" at the address above.

Build YOUR Space/ Julie Sawchuk. —1st ed.

ISBN 978-1-9992384-0-7

# Contents

*Dedicated to Dean O'Reilly*

*Home is wherever I'm with you.*
—Edward Sharpe & the Magnetic Zeros

# Foreword

By *Rick Hansen, Founder, Rick Hansen Foundation*

I RECALL HOW daunting it was as a 16-year-old returning home for the first time after my accident. It was the end of one battle and the beginning of another. While I had built up my strength fairly quickly – I could walk on braces and crutches and I could scoot around in a wheelchair, that didn't change the fact that my home was totally inaccessible.

My dad had created a space for me in the basement, but there were stairs to get down to my room. I bum-hitched up and down the stairs and I'd attempt to pull myself along the handrails, but I'd put so much pressure on them that they'd rip right out of the bannister and I'd be sent tumbling head first and backwards down the landing. I fought the house, and the house also fought back.

Living in an accessible space is ultimately about independence. When we don't have to spend our energy fighting with our space, we suddenly free ourselves up for not only the activities we enjoy doing, but the simple things that others might take for granted like loading the dishwasher or taking a cup of coffee onto the patio. An accessible home provides us with the freedom to participate fully in life.

In 1974, when I returned home from rehab there were limited to no resources for my family to reference when they tried to make our home accessible. Forty plus years later, I know Julie Sawchuk also struggled to find the resources she needed, so she set out to create her own. As a designated Rick Hansen Foundation Accessibility Certification Professional, Julie was empowered to apply her training to build her dream home to be wheelchair accessible. *Build YOUR Space* is a constructive reference guide filled with Universal Design-inspired solutions for building an accessible living space.

In *Build YOUR Space*, Julie has compiled stories from her personal experience, but also the lived experience of those that have navigated renovations for their condo, mobile home or even Tiny Home and customized it to suit their accessibility needs. Julie provides a thoughtful planning checklist of considerations to barriers, but also practical solutions that will help anyone living with, or caring for, someone with a disability to safely achieve independence in their home.

Prior to her accident, Julie was a teacher and it's no surprise that she continues to share her passion for teaching through her advocacy for accessibility. She shows us that building for access is much more than eliminating stairs or complying to building codes; it's about creating meaningful access so that your home can adapt to you and your family's changing needs through the course of your lifetime.

# Preface

I HAD THE PRIVILEGE of the use of my legs for the first 42 years of my life. What happened next left me using a wheelchair from that point on. Now, I get it. I understand why access allows for freedom, personal energy conservation and inclusion. This book is designed to help you and your architect, interior designer and builder understand why properly planned accessibility makes a world of difference.

As we were building our own completely wheelchair accessible home, we realized that we needed to document the process. We learned so much – we had never built a house before, let alone one designed for wheelchair access. There are a million tiny things to consider, and not just counter height and turning radius!

As we planned and started to build, we struggled to find resources to help us make those million decisions. That is where *Build YOUR Space* was born. I decided to write down everything that we learned so that others would benefit and have an easier time with their own project.

I invite you to read this book from cover to cover; however, how you use it depends on where you are in the process of designing or building your accessible home. Please also keep in mind that although I write from the perspective of a manual wheelchair user, you will be able to see how your own type of mobility device and physical needs can be considered.

Chapter 1 tells my story. It explains why we needed first to renovate our old farmhouse, and then why we decided to build a brand-new home. Chapter 2 will help you through the planning process and Chapter 3 will help open your eyes to all the little things that add up to make a big difference. If you are already in the throes of renovating or building and need the "checklist" of things to think about, then go to Chapters 4 and 5 for house and room specific needs.

Chapter 6 will help you think "outside the box" for accessible living ideas like mobile access and condo living. You'll also read about others who learned from their own experiences and wanted to share. The end of the book contains a list of additional resources that will help you get your project done.

We would not have such a wonderful home were it not for all the people who helped just by listening. I had many conversations with those involved – many of whom had never been a part of an accessible home project. We learned together, and that requires being vulnerable. I had to explain the specifics of my needs and they had to recognize that they needed to learn how to make it all work. It was not easy – but we did it and so can you.

## A NOTE ABOUT UNITS OF MEASURE

Even though Canada is a country that officially uses metric measurements, I have found that both the design and construction industries use the Imperial system. Because of this, I have chosen to use Imperial measurements for all my width and height suggestions.

# Acknowledgements

WE HAD AN AMAZING team of people work together to help create our magnificent space. I'd like to thank them all for the extra time and effort they put into making our home a showcase of accessibility. Were it not for your thoughtful consideration of all my needs, I would not be leading the productive life that I now have.

The project started with the design team of Elizabeth Laing, Margaret McColl and Graham Whiting from Whiting Design (Waterloo, Ontario). They had the arduous task of tolerating the many changes to our plans (30+ versions!). Their architectural drawings are what brought this build to life.

The lay of the land here is relatively flat, which created challenges for slope and drainage. The folks from Culbert Surveying, together with Bruinsma Excavating (Goderich) and concrete foundation expert Mike Siertsema of Supreme Concrete (Blyth) put the house foundation in exactly the right location, angle and height.

Our builder, Casey Boven of CMB Construction in Blyth, managed our build with skill and really took the time to ask questions and listen to explanations. His team of Mike Yantzi, Chris Stewart and Trevor DeCourte were "in the loop" about making small changes that made a big difference for accessibility.

Larry & Cindy Morrison of L&M Concrete in Clinton poured a perfectly level cement floor and Lorne Teataro (from Brucefield) laid the glued-down vinyl plank. I can sit in my chair, without my brakes on, and not move!

Advantage Insulation (Kyle Wheeler and Tom MacDonald) of Lucknow filled this house with the super efficient Blow-in-Blanket insulation system. We have NO drafts!

Gentek Windows & Doors, MacDonald Lumber (Home Hardware Brussels) provided all of the building supplies.

Clinton Roof & Truss gave us shelter and Whitestone Inc. (of Forest) installed the most beautiful raised-seam steel roof – people stop to ask us about it because they want one too. Ed Stein of Ed's Siding and Eavestrough gave it the finishing touch.

Geotech Plumbing and Heating installed the geothermal heat, in-floor heating and airflow system. Cool air that falls from above and warmth from the floor – it works so well for us all!

Wayne Smith of KMN Smith Electrical (Clinton) and Scott Townsend of Townsend Plumbing (Vanastra) understood how reducing reach improved access. Wayne had new ideas (like turning the electrical panel to be horizontal) and Scott brought years of experience.

Cindy Kerr from iDesigns (Listowel) made all our kitchen dreams become a reality and Thomas Dykstra of The Cabinet Guys (also from Listowel) put it all together – everything is so smooth. They even went so far as to return some materials to the factory to round the edges of counters and posts on the island. The butcher block is my favorite space to sit, visit and work!

The most comfortable place in the bathroom is my shower bench. I thank Brent and his crew from R&R Machine & Tool in Teeswater for designing and building the bench and Dorothy at Barmy Tech for the waterproof cushion and cover. I could shower for hours...

The final piece of a new build is always the landscaping. Paul VanderMolen, owner of The LawnMaster (Seaforth), was a part of this project from the beginning. He and his hardworking team have created an outdoor space that is the envy of all. I have access to gardens and can roll (my body) on the lawn.

It would be unfair for me to say that all these amazing accessible home ideas were mine – they are not. They came from all the friends who built homes before and after me. Dave Wilsie, Lorie Falconer, Shannon Wilcox, Ralph Wood, Cody Caldwell, Debbie Kerley, Craig Lenz, Michelle Seringer, Megan Woodiwiss, Julie Watson and of course, Chris Fraser. Touring friends' accessible homes became my mission for several years. All those visits paid off, so THANK YOU!

Moving from one house to another is never easy. Here, we have our new house beside our old one; you'd think it would be easier. But it's not! Thank you to Elaine Delisle (the other half of my brain) and Heather Snell (the declutter/cleaning machine) for all the hours and hours they spent helping us.

As for the production of this book, I thank my Publisher Suzanne Doyle-Ingram from Prominence Publishing. When I first connected with Suzanne, I knew she would help me do great things; first *Shine Volume 3 – Inspirational Stories of Overcoming Adversity*, and now *Build YOUR Space* is done too! I also want to thank my dear friend, fellow educator and now editor, Vicki McDonald. She stepped up without hesitation to help me get this project finished and from her I learned grammar lessons that I now dream about!

Photo credits go to Heather Dietz de Boer of Blyth. Although she is a professional wedding photographer, she offered her services to capture all the nuances of our home and bring them to life on paper for you to see.

Lastly, I thank my husband, Theo. Standing at 6'3" and me forever now seated, we make an odd-looking couple, but also the perfect one to showcase Universal Design. Our stature made compromise on some things (like counter height) difficult, but it also gives us a collective perspective that there is no one-size-fits-all solution. But we did it, and it works for our family.

It took way longer to plan than we had wished for, but that time gave us the insights that made this house as beautiful and functional as it is. Were it not for his patience, kindness, and love in the last 25 years and his willingness to stick it out over the last

four, I'm not sure where we would be. His capacity for hope has carried us through as a family, and allowed me to have the opportunity to bring this book to you.

# Why physical accessibility is a priority

## Where all this began

ON JULY 29TH, 2015, I was hit from behind by a car while I was riding my bike. I was thrown 30 feet into the ditch and sustained life-threatening injuries. The worst of those injuries were two fractured vertebrae, T4 and L1. The T4 vertebra ruptured and shot a fragment of bone into my spinal column, causing an in-complete spinal cord injury (SCI) and paralysis from the chest down. I would no longer have the use of my legs. From that day forward I have been using a manual wheelchair for mobility. I was 42 years old at the time.

I was (and still am) married to Theo and with our two kids, Ella and Oliver, we have a small farm (10 acres) outside the Village of Blyth in Southwestern Ontario. On that ten acres we have (had) a 110-year-old farmhouse. We bought it with an eye to the future – a true "fixer-upper". We had been working away at it as time and money would allow. We didn't know when we bought it that we would tear it down 11 years later.

Old Ontario farmhouses tend not to be wheelchair friendly, and this one was no exception. The original home had a total of four additions. This means that on top of the four steps to get into the house, there were four other "levels" that each needed to be ramped so I could have access to those spaces, including the entry, family room and office. And that did not include the second floor, which is where our kids' bedrooms were. I deliberately put quotes around the word "levels" because nothing was level in that house. You could drop marbles in the middle and they would all roll somewhere different. It was not an easy way to live on wheels – everything required more physical energy. For example, getting something from the fridge: I would open the fridge door, lean forward, reach forward and roll backward... I had to put my brakes on just to get the milk!

At the time of publication, this old house was still standing. But it won't be for long. Living here was hard, but we made it work. When we started to move over to the new house, all sorts of stuff came down from upstairs – things that I had forgotten we even had!

## COMING HOME

*Two months into my four-month hospital stay I came home for a weekend. My husband and his friends had moved our bed to the main floor to make our new bedroom, the former dining room. Other furniture had been moved to give me space to get around, but it was tight. Aside from all the physical discomfort I was still experiencing, the emotional toll of coming home hit me hard. I would never be able to walk around our property independently, enjoy the trees and help with our large vegetable and fruit gardens. Even travelling up and down the long gravel driveway would forever depend on the season and the weather. At a time that should have been joyful, coming home really hit hard.*

But we made it work. I came home to our farm after four months in hospital. With help from our contractor friend Casey, they built a ramp, removed some cupboards in the kitchen and created a roll-in shower in the bathroom. When I became a bit more independent, we added some grab bars to the walls beside the toilet. Thank goodness our bathroom was on the first floor; that is not always the case in old farmhouses.

In the meantime, there were all sorts of insurance and legal things to figure out. Ontario Auto Insurance is set out to help those with catastrophic injuries from motor vehicle accidents (MVA) recover to the best "normal" life possible. This was where the money would come from to build our new, accessible home. We had quotes for renovating the farmhouse, but they were up to $800,000! Some quotes even included installing an elevator, but in the end we knew that even if we had a lovely addition that was accessible and had a roll-in shower, we'd still have an old farm house with a wet basement and a roof that was going to need to be replaced.

That was when we started making plans to build a new house. Because we have ten acres, space was not really an issue, but we still had the constraints of the water well and hydro line location, so we couldn't be too far away from the old house. We

3

briefly thought about tearing down and then building, but then we'd have nowhere to live! If we were to go this route, we would have had to find an accessible place to live for almost a year, but in our village and in all the surrounding towns there is nothing without a step, narrow doors and tiny bathrooms. So, we decided to stay put and start planning to build.

## This book is for you

What do you do when you start a project that is going to cost you hundreds of thousands of dollars? Research. I needed a book, a resource, a guide and some checklists for building an accessible home. Building Code manuals and various types of bungalow home plans were not enough. There are so many things to consider! What I learned is that there was no guide for building a wheelchair accessible home – but now there is, and you are reading it! This book is for you – so you don't have to do all the "leg" work that we did before we built.

The new kitchen is fantastic, with plenty of space and a great view out the low windows. One thing that was hard to compromise was the height of the rangehood – in the end it was within range of my reach, but also Theo's forehead!

I wrote this book because you, or someone you love, has a need for access. Maybe you have a child who has a physical disability and now that he is growing, he needs more space and you need to change the setup of your home? Perhaps your parent had a stroke and now has partial paralysis? Are you a wheelchair user and need to make changes to the place where you live? Are you ready to do it right? Are you tired of consuming all your energy just for daily living? Do you want to learn how to set up a bathroom for guests? Do you ever think, "Why can't people do this right?" Now you can and now is the time. Don't wait to make changes; don't wait to build. Start your planning now. This is your manual for doing it right.

## Few and far between

Information about building for access is hard to find. Resources are few and the experience of people in the industry is less. I have learned that architects, builders and designers spend little time during their education learning about accessibility and Universal Design. We learned that we needed to be our own experts. We had to put bits and pieces together from each home we visited. Every time I met someone who had an accessible home, I'd ask to visit and take pictures and measurements. I also made notes of what I liked best and what didn't work for me.

This book has all the information that we learned, all together, in one place. I want you to have a smoother ride as you go on your journey to build (or renovate) for access. The principles of Universal Design (UD) are key to creating an accessible home for yourself. There are a few good resources out there for UD; you can even take a whole degree in UD! (See Appendix.)

When you use the principles of Universal Design to build your space, everyone wins, even those who choose a "RipStik" to get around the house.

There are also resources like the Ontario Building Code (OBC), BUT those guidelines are also for commercial properties where all people are to have full access to every space. Building your own home means you get to do it your way. Don't ignore the OBC, but use it as a guideline. In your home you can put the grab bars exactly where you need them.

You don't know what your life will be like down the road. As you read through this book, you can "think forward" to when you may find yourself needing an accessible space. According to the Rick Hansen Foundation, by 2036 one in five people in Canada will identify as having a disability and 50% of the population currently has a relationship with someone with a disability. In 2019 the Canadian Parliament passed National Accessibility Standards! We are slowly moving forward in this country!

## Our home is amazing

We moved in on December 22, 2018. The difference between life in a 110-year-old, two-storey farmhouse and our single-storey, universally designed home is like night and day. My energy levels are higher. My ability to participate in all aspects of our household has returned. I cook and bake. I have the energy and ability to shower when I want to, not just every other day (with assistance). Getting in and out of the house is a breeze and I have an outdoor space that is easy for me to access. I hope that next year I'll even be able to garden!

I have been showing our home to anyone who is interested and even some who are just curious! It's become my new classroom, a "living laboratory" of accessibility. Sure, there are a few things that I would do differently now that we have been living here for a few months, but everything works for me, my family and my friends who come to visit. We have space to entertain, play games and sometimes even be messy! Consider this book your invitation to come and see it for yourself.

This photo of the front entry shows the level threshold and the Unilock on the front patio. The pattern in the flooring is not carpet – it is the same vinyl plank as the rest of the house.

We choose a door with three panels of glass and a sidelight to let a lot of natural light into the space. The bench is there for those who need to sit to put their shoes on and off.

At the time, we didn't realize that the lower glass panel was perfect cat height! "Let me in!"

## ACCESS DOES NOT EQUAL UGLY

*You need to know that accessible does not mean ugly. An accessible home does not mean massive ramps, institutional grab bars and gadgets everywhere. Homes that are accessible, that are designed with everyone in mind, can also be beautiful. Of the many people who have come to see our new home my favourite comment is "If I didn't know you, I never would have known this home was designed for a wheelchair user." Bam! That was*

*our goal. Make it right, but make it beautiful*
*at the same time.*

## Chapter 1: Summary

- ❏ As a wheelchair user, Julie has lived through the experience of renovating and building.
- ❏ You and your people need resources to help you through this process – this is your guide.
- ❏ Planning with universal design means everyone gets to access all spaces in your home with comfort and safety.
- ❏ You will find photos and diagrams to help you imagine your future space.
- ❏ This book will help you design for you, your loved ones and your future!
- ❏ Accessible can be beautiful as well as functional.

CHAPTER 2

# Planning pays off

## Before you start

VISIT, VISIT, VISIT. Ask your friends and relations, "Who do you know that has an accessible home?" Then go! You will develop an understanding of what you like, and more importantly what you don't like, or doesn't work for you. There is no "one-size-fits-all" prescription. Standard built-for-accessibility building code is not applied in the same way when you build a home. You still must meet minimum code standards for things like fire safety and energy conservation, but not access. Access standards like turning radius apply only to public spaces.

Perhaps you are renovating because you don't want to move. That's okay! You will make it work and the more you visit and learn what works for you, the easier that will be to get it right. By seeing other homes, you will have rolled under lots of sinks, tried elevators, roll-in showers and checked out lots of closet organizing systems. You need to see it, try it, experience it. That is how you are going to know what you like. That is how you are going to make your home awesome!

## Why does access matter?

My ultimate goal was complete independence. I am one stubborn woman and I wanted to be able to do everything on my own. In the old farmhouse I had to have help maneuvering my wheelchair while I had a shower because our bathroom was not

9

big enough for my chair and my shower commode. I also had to roll through the kitchen (usually dripping wet) to get dried and dressed in the bedroom – not a very dignified way to start the day.

I love to cook. In the old house, it was a very energy-consuming thing to do, and also not always safe when you can't see into the pot! The kitchen was so tiny I had to stay in one spot, or my family would have injured toes.

The other aspect of poor access is inclusion. In the old house I often felt not included. It wasn't intentional, but my kids were upstairs, and I could not join them. For three and a half years they said goodnight to me downstairs. It's a hard thing for a mother not to be able to say goodnight to her kids, pull up the covers and tuck them in. I also missed sneaking in after they were asleep and watching them, peaceful and young. It made me sad. Add to that the frustration of trying to wake them up in the morning from the bottom of the stairs! It's only right for all family members to be included in all aspects of family life.

After they completed some major renovations, my physio clinic (Glassier Physiotherapy), had a space that was "just my height". I felt like Goldilocks at a counter that was built for me. This is when you need your measuring tape handy!

## Start planning with numbers

Use the chart below to help you determine your measurements. Reach sideways, forward and from a "side saddle" position. Remember that your reach forward will be different depending on whether you can roll under, and lean on a surface. As you shop and try things out in stores, as you visit friends' homes and as you read books, take pictures. I carry a tape measure around with me (in my backpack) wherever I go. One day you will roll up to a counter that you love (in a store or at an office) and you'll want to know the exact height. Take a picture, record the height and apply it to your kitchen and bathroom and in your personal workspace.

| Number to know for your mobility device | Example from Julie's wheelchair | Your numbers |
|---|---|---|
| Tight turning radius | 38" | |
| Width of device | 25" | |
| Seated knee clearance | 26.5" | |
| Sideways reach | 33" | |
| Forward reach (seated with knees under) | 25" | |
| Forward reach (seated without knees under) | 21" | |
| Maximum height reach | 62" | |
| | | |

## Keep track and save!

For each decision you make – from counter height to wall colour – write it down in a notebook. Create files (paper and electronic) to keep track of all your ideas and invoices. File pictures you pull from magazines and plans you have sketched out. Keep all receipts and invoices as you may be able to get some tax write-offs for building an accessible home. In Ontario, this may also apply to your property assessment. Ask your accountant to help you with this – it can make a significant difference.

As your invoices start to roll in, have your builder, electrician, cabinet maker and floor layer write on their invoice what they did to make your home accessible. Wide doorways, flush floor, lower countertops, lower windows, level driveway with poured cement, sunken door frames... All these things are what the tax folks will recognize and appreciate when reviewing your assessment.

## Don't rush (if you can help it)

Please don't be scared by this, but we took over two years to plan and build our new home! Part of it was being stalled by seasons and weather, but part of it was indecision. In the end, it was worth the wait because we were able to build in the summer months (rather than fall/winter). We also made changes to the kitchen layout by adding the pantry and removing high cabinets. While we were in the planning stages, I stayed the night and used the roll-in shower at my friend Chris's house – cooking in her kitchen and parking in her garage. It all made a difference in our design. We were going to push to start the build sooner, but the plans didn't feel ready, and neither were we.

That extra year also gave me more time to recover. With a spinal cord injury there is no way to predict how much strength and sensation you will regain. No matter what doctors may say, they do not know. I recovered more core strength than anyone would have guessed. This has given me more "flexibility" in how I use the bathroom and how independently I function around the house. I acquired some specialized exercise equipment that needed space and I also had time to discover that I can sew with a regular sewing machine (a former hobby) and therefore needed the space to set up and store fabrics.

## Practice

As you go from floor plans to vertical sketches, set up mock layouts so you can experiment with turning radius, width of hallways, knee clearance and height of windows. Draw the walls with chalk or tape, add a box or bucket to simulate the sink and toilet and then you may begin to discover you need more room to maneuver your wheelchair, walker or scooter. You can do this just about anywhere – church basement, driveway, or parking lot – but do it! As you "enter" each space you may realize that perhaps you need to add another 8-12"; remember to take notes and lots of pictures.

## Build for NOW

*Build YOUR Space* is for YOU, not for the next owners. One thing we went back and forth with was counter height. What if we needed to sell the house and prospective buyers didn't like the look of lower counter space?

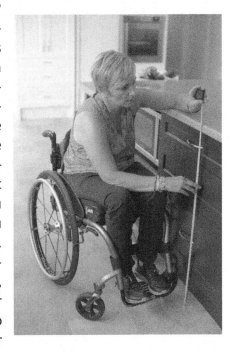

Too bad! Even if we sell before we die, the new owners are likely going to change a bunch of things anyway. Besides, once you set up a couple of stools, you'll realize that everyone can enjoy the lower workspace – it will become your new breakfast nook. Focus on what you need now and what you might want for your future. Think about electrical outlets in the ceiling for a lift, backing behind drywall for future grab bars and easy to pull out drawers for all your storage.

## No basement? Where's your stuff?

It was a hard concept, at first. Where do the "guts" of the house go? What about all the stuff that we store down there? No basement means the first level of the house is at ground level; it's called "slab on grade". This method means there is no need for steps or ramps. There is also no basement to worry about leaking – which in the Ontario mid-winter and spring thaws is always a concern.

We located the electrical panel in the garage and turned it horizontally, making it easy to reach all switches. The furnace, hot water heater and water softener are in a maintenance room on the main floor. This room was made soundproof with insulation and a solid door. Vibrations were controlled with a special panel. The 10′ x 10′ is tight, but it is enough space to house all the equipment in a way that I can access.

In this photo you can see a few different aspects of the beginning of the build: the foundation walls, the cut-out for the front door, the water pipes coming up through the gravel, the vapour barrier and the Styrofoam insulation. What you don't see is the basement – because there isn't one!

## Budget

By far this is the hardest thing to do. Set your budget and tell everyone involved what your limit is. Start with it up front and then your designer and your contractor will be able to guide you through the costs of building materials and square foot costs to help you make decisions and prioritize your spending. Building for accessibility does not have to cost more; it's the size of your home that will really make a difference. Remember to include the cost of landscaping; even if you choose a simple front walk of paving stone, it still costs money! Check with your builder to see if they will look after organizing the landscaping to be done after the build is finished – it's often a forgotten expense.

## Assemble your team

The focus of this book is on the aspects that are required for wheelchair access following the principles of Universal Design. The design and construction ideas discussed in this book are for everyone, no matter what stage in life or ability. You will still need to seek out other building resources to help you decide things like what kind of roofing, countertop material and paint colours. I am not an architect or a designer. I am not a building code specialist. I am an accessibility strategist with the lived experience that will guide you to find solutions that work best for you. The following is a list of people you will need to help guide you through the whole process. Whenever possible, find people who have experience working with and designing for accessibility.

*NO EXPERIENCE REQUIRED*
*When we started our quest for the right building design team, I had it in my head that we needed to find the experts. We didn't know what we were doing, so we needed someone to tell us. In the end, what I think worked better was having a team that was willing to learn about building for access. They saw it as a new skill to have in their portfolio. Sitting down together to discuss kitchen designs, locating where the backing would go in the bathrooms and how to make doorways better meant that we learned together. Each one of us had to be vulnerable, recognize that we didn't know what to do and find solutions together. That is how we accomplished our dreams.*

This is my favourite picture from the photo shoot Heather Dietz did for this book. It perfectly captures one of those great moments of "life".

You can see the natural light coming in the south-facing windows and the pantry behind me. It shows the butcher block, my favourite workspace, and I have my lapboard ready for my hot mid-morning coffee.

What you don't see is the funny conversation Oliver and I are having – you can tell by the rise of his cheekbones!

## *Banker/Money manager/Accountant*

Sit down with your money person and have an honest conversation with them about how much you have available to you. Whether you have an insurance payout from an accident (like me) or are using a mortgage, you need to communicate how much you have to spend. I knew we had the money needed to build, but if I had known then what I know now, I would have approached it differently. That honest conversation never really happened for us and instead we just plowed our way into the project.

Remember to always add more, at least 10% more, for the "unforeseen" expenses. Hydro One made us run a new electrical service up the 300' driveway to account for the new building code electricity regulations. We also purchased a propane generator to supply electricity during power outages. We also didn't account for purchasing new furniture.

## Architect/Designer

Aside from having the money lined up, your architect is who is really going to get the ball rolling. Choose wisely and make sure you have seen their work; you need to work together to create a vision that makes sense for you both. Talk about what they know about accessibility and how willing they are to learn more. Communication about timelines is paramount. Knowing what you want before you start is key, so use the later sections of this book to help you make decisions about what your priority is for maximizing space. Use pictures of the places you have visited to show your designer what you have in mind, what you like and what you don't like. Ask for references and speak to those former clients. If you start without a clear vision this process will take longer (and cost more) so be sure you know what you want.

---

### IN THE DRIVER'S SEAT

*When you build or renovate you will be forking out a lot of money, not just for materials but to pay people. You have got to be satisfied with their work. You are the one signing the cheques so you should be in control. Do not let yourself be intimidated; be brave enough to stand up for what you want. If you are not happy, say so.*

---

## General Contractor

This is the person who will be responsible for organizing and timing the work that goes on. From cement work to framing and trusses, plumbing and electrical, drywall and painting, windows and doors, flooring and kitchen installation – they will lay out the timelines and book in the work. In the meantime, you need to have a frank discussion with your contractor about space and proper placement of things like grab bars, shower heads, toilet location... it will likely get personal! It's often the "behind the scenes" things that makes the biggest difference – stuff you don't even know you need until you need it! Installing ¾" or 1" plywood backing around the toilet, shower or bathtub is essential if you decide to put up grab bars now or in the future.

Help your contractor understand EXACTLY WHY things (like the toilet) need to go EXACTLY WHERE you say they do. It becomes a discussion of personal energy conservation and safety. During our build, the inside bathroom wall got shifted an inch. This meant that the toilet was slightly farther from the wall than it was meant to be. This caused transfers to and from the toilet to my wheelchair to require more shoulder strength and balance. We fixed it by moving the grab bar out from the wall. My point is that every inch makes a big difference.

### Kitchen designer/Installer

Take the time to go to the kitchen design company and meet face to face. The design room is a great place to test out countertop edges (you'll want a rounded edge as it's easier on your forearms) and test heights of counters, reach for sinks, drawer style, Lazy Susan, types of drawer pulls (D pulls are most accessible), as well as the fun things like colour.

Take your list of accessibility requirements and leave it with them. Be very specific and check in regularly. Rounded corners in the kitchen (like the corners of your island) are things to think about adding to your list. It hurts to run into a sharp corner! See the Kitchen section (Chapter 5) for more details and help creating your kitchen list.

The beginning of the island! If you look at the base, you can see two heights for the kickplates. The right side I will be able to roll up to and tuck my toes underneath. Designed in two pieces meant that we could run electrical down the middle for lights and outlets.

## Plumber & Electrician

Be involved with each of these team members before they come on site. Have those same face-to-face, personal conversations about your needs. Explain where your furniture will be placed (i.e. beds) and which doors you'll use most often. This way, electrical outlets and switches go where they are needed. Show the plumber how you approach a work surface, so they know how to avoid plumbing fixtures and drains from coming into contact with your feet, legs and especially your knees. Explain why the depth of the sink or the location of the light switches really matters. See Chapter 4 for more details about plumbing and electrical considerations.

# Industry Expert: From the Builder

This section of the book gives you perspectives from Casey Boven of CMB Construction, the custom home builder whose team built our new and wonderful home. I interviewed Casey after our home was finished. We sat at the kitchen table and talked about what we learned from this project. Here is what he had to say:

*What was the "biggest take away" from building your first completely accessible home?*

Building a custom home is one thing; you are using the owner's life savings to build the home of their dreams. When we built this home, it was for a different type of dream; accessibility is about quality of life, not just lifestyle. Quality of life is not a luxury!

I learned from Julie that small issues are magnified when you have a disability – like the little bumps in floor finishes or changes in thresholds. We installed a rubber lip in her old house as a temporary solution for a roll-in shower for Julie. Even though it folds down, what I didn't realize was that it was still high enough to cause problems. The little details can be overlooked; they are super specific for each individual – which is why communication is so important.

The day the trusses arrived was pretty exciting – not just because they were here, but because the driver backed the truck up the driveway and around the 90° corner to the new house without going in the ditch!

*When it comes to standard installations like water, heat and hydro, were there any major differences?*

Yes! Hot water temperatures should be modified for people with a lack of temperature sensation in their skin. Burns can happen without realizing it. Drainpipes should be covered or wrapped and sink bottoms far enough away from knees that there can be no heat transfer. Hydro breaker panels should be installed at a height that still meets code but can be reached by everyone. Simply turning the panel horizontally made that happen. We also lowered the light switches and raised the outlets – you can't even tell.

The most significant change in my thinking about "standard installs" was learning about how home heating affects people with spinal cord injury or other nerve disorders. Fluctuations in room temperature (like what happens with ducted air flow) can cause a lot of discomfort. What Julie learned was how much better she felt living in a space with even heat (from in-floor heating).

*Where there any major differences to the structure or foundation?*

We bumped up the load restrictions on the trusses for the bathroom and master bedroom. In the future, there may be a need for a lift track or transfer equipment for Julie as she ages. Setting the trusses to hold more weight means that they can do that without worry.

Standard exterior doors were used, but we made alterations before we poured the foundation. We inset the doors into the concrete wall foundations so that the transition from inside to outside was minimal. It's also important that you know well in advance the specs of anything that is different; Julie installed an indoor, inground pool so we needed to know the exact size of the opening in order for the edge to be flush with the floor.

*Did Julie's house require a lot of "bells and whistles"? Were their extra costs?*

Small, simple changes were needed for accessibility. Having no "upper" kitchen cabinets meant that Julie could reach everything. We added a pantry instead – not exactly a luxury, but it is big so that added square footage to the design. Level thresholds required more pre-planning (with the foundation installer) but did not require different materials – we used standard doors.

Having no changes in flooring throughout the house actually made it easier to install. Pocket doors are of value for saving space; the doors cost a bit more than a regular door and they require a bit more labour for installation, but in total they only added $150 (i.e. for the pantry door).

Anything that the builder can do to make a client's life, day, hour better is worth it for you, not just getting in and getting done so you can move on to the next house. It's about doing all the little details to make it right.

*The roll-in shower is fantastic – tell us how you did it.*

It's important to start out knowing which floor finishes you are using because you need to know the exact heights. We used a linear drain instead of a circle drain so that it slopes in only one direction. One-way slope also means equipment, like a shower chair, sits flat on the floor, as opposed to slopes in multiple directions that might make a chair unstable.

The drain assembly was installed, then the plastic pan that was already pre-sloped was next. We use the self-leveling concrete to pour the 5' x 5' space – it was not poured when the rest of the floor was done. (see photo) The self-leveler was poured to a height that would accommodate the shower pan and tile so it would be the same height as the floor. The floor tile is not polished, so it's not slippery when wet.

This is the day Casey installed the shower bench – the day we realized we didn't put the backer low enough, which made things a bit more complicated!

We also added backer everywhere behind the wall tile; that way additions like a shower bench and grab bars can be installed pretty much anywhere. We wish we had added backer in more places where equipment and grab bars may be installed in the future. Simply adding 1" plywood behind the drywall means  anything can go anywhere.

*Did you need to know more about your client for this project, compared to other builds?*

Absolutely. It helped that we were already friends, but I certainly did not already know all of the inside information about life with paralysis. We had to be comfortable having conversations about things like toilet transfers, showering and getting dressed. Communication was key to making all the little things right, because little things make a big difference. Building for access means trying to make the client's life as close as before, like access to outdoor living, or space to work safely in the kitchen. You want to make their life richer. Doing this emphasizes the importance of having all those conversations before you start and as the build goes along.

## What do you love about the final product?

All the windows brighten the house; they bring positive energy, colour, natural light and all this improves the mood of the home. The other aspect that I love is that it does not look like an accessible home. It just looks beautiful and you'd never know it was "different" from a regular build.

## Is there anything to watch out for, like gimmicky accessibility things?

Some companies make accessible door sills – these door frame features may not be best for the climate, i.e. rain, snow and wind. The concept of a "smart home" (everything connected to your phone) is good, but it's not necessary. Placing climate controls and electrical panels low enough to be reached is all that's needed.

## What "accessible home" design advice would you give architects?

Extra space in the hallways – clear free space of 72" – so that passing in the hallway or kitchen is easy. Add little things like a "drop zone" shelf beside the fridge, lots of pullouts and drawers.

Whenever you think you have enough space in the kitchen ADD MORE. Eliminating upper cabinets means you need more storage, but also gives you the opportunity to add windows!

*Any final advice for builders?*

Having the right team to work together was really important. We used the expertise of others so things could be done right. For example, the orientation of the house and the height of the foundation required a lot of communication with the surveyors. We wanted the water to run away from the house, but at the same time we did not want to create unmanageable slopes. Minimize corners if possible. I see now how corners get run into with a wheelchair!

Communication with your sub-trades is essential. Explain decisions from the point of view of the client, especially if there is a language barrier between sub-trades; take the time to interpret and emphasize the differences from a standard build. You have to explain why things are being done differently, and that it has to be done the way the client has requested, because it's for a reason (like sink depth). Your workers need to not automatically assume that they are going to do things the way they have always done them.

Don't assume. There is no such thing as a dumb question; when in doubt clarify with your client.

---

*NO SUCH THING AS TOO MUCH BACKER*
*"Backer" is the term used by builders to describe the wood that is used to grab screws that go through drywall. These screws are usually holding up things like towel bars and*

*shelves. But where backer becomes essential is when it is used to hold up weight-bearing things like grab bars and shower benches. When we were building the master bathroom, we thought we had it all covered. We planned where we thought the shower bench would go and where the grab bars would be now, and in the future. Then they put up the walls and tiled them.*

*At the time, I had not ordered my shower bench. If I had had it while we were doing the*

*planning, we would have seen that the screws that hold the bottom bracket in place are almost at floor level... which is where we didn't put backer. Why would you need backer that low to the floor, anyway? When I finally did get my shower bench and Casey went to install it, we realized (when we looked back at the photos we took) there was no backer where we needed it to be. The result? Casey went through the drywall on the other side of the wall to install backer that would hold my seat firmly in place. No big*

*deal; it got the job done, but I really thought*
*we were done with drywall dust!*

---

## Make YOUR home a show home

There are not many built with access as a priority, so tell your team that you want to be able to show off your space and that it's possible to build for accessibility, safety and personal energy conservation all rolled into one. If building a show home is not your thing, just build with the confidence that you have done everything you need to build YOUR best home.

### *Chapter 2: Summary*

- ❏ Failing to plan is planning to fail – it takes time and energy but is so very necessary.
- ❏ Visit other homes that have been designed for access.
- ❏ Have a budget and stick to it. Don't be afraid to say how much or how little you have to spend. It's important for your peace of mind.
- ❏ Set up a space where you can try things out to see how they feel, like counter height.
- ❏ Hire people who have experience with accessibility and Universal Design – have them show you their work and have face-to-face discussions explaining your needs.
- ❏ Build for where you are at now, but plan for the future.

# CHAPTER 3

# Little decisions that made a BIG difference

## Identify your needs

THE BIGGEST THING you have to gain (other than safety) is energy, personal energy. When you live in a space that is designed for you specifically, you can reduce the number of energy units you spend each day. As we were building, my friend Lorie kept telling me what a big difference this house would make for my energy levels every day. I knew she was right, and that life would be better, but it wasn't until after we moved in that I realized just how right she was! I felt like a new person! I could fit more things into my days and I (sometimes) even managed to stay up later than my kids. Here are some examples from my current situation:

- A higher toilet requires less lift and leverage when transferring.
- My properly angled shower bench means I don't have to hold myself up with one hand and wash my hair with the other.
- I have space to move around the dishwasher while it's open and it doesn't have to be closed to get into the kitchen.

- The pantry allows me to reach everything that I need without overextending.
- Level floors and wide doorways make travel faster and save my knuckles.
- The roll-under cooktop means I can cook what I want, safely.

Someday I want to host a cooking show in my beautiful, accessible kitchen!

In your current living situation, where do you expend more energy than necessary? Make a list and share it with your architect and contractor. As you go through it together, discuss what you can do to make changes.

My list (while living in my old farmhouse) would look something like this:

- Ramps up into the house and within the house between levels require extra energy and balance
- Narrow doorways injure fingers
- Carpeted entry is hard to move on

- No turning radius in entry means multipoint turns to get in/out of the house
- The small bathroom means transferring and pushing chair out into the kitchen to have a shower
- Uneven floors require putting my brakes on and off just to stay in one place in the kitchen/bathroom
- Reaching for dishes and ingredients in the kitchen is often difficult/requires help
- Getting in and out of the car in the snow and rain means my seat cushion gets damp

You get the idea – go through your day and *actually list* every action that you take that could be done in a way that consumes less of your energy.

## Type of mobility device

How do you get around? Do have a small manual wheelchair, a power chair, walker, cane or scooter? Maybe you have a combination of all of the above? Whatever it is that you use to help you get around, plan for the space they take up and think ahead to how your mobility device may change in the future. Scooters need parking space and larger turning radii. Like power wheelchairs, they also need to have designated charging stations. What is the turning radius of your current mobility device? Where do you normally park your wheels? Where do you wish you could park them? In your current home, what space are you not able to get into/travel through? Where do you transfer from one space to another?

Right now, you may have a small manual chair which may make it seem that you don't need a lot of space to get around. Circumstances change. In the future, you may require a larger mobility device with a larger turning radius. Plan for it in your design – in doorways, the hall, bathrooms, the mudroom and the kitchen. If possible, make sure you are able to get around the dishwasher when it is open. Hallways should be at least 4' wide, but 5' is best.

Sketch out your current living space and draw on your current problems. Share it with your designer and talk about how your setup could change to minimize effort, travel time, trips back and forth, and so that you can get everywhere. One example from our farmhouse of an inaccessible space was our bedroom. I was not able to reach the only window that opened. Because of the transfer space I needed on my side of the bed, Theo's side was almost right next to the wall, making the window out of reach for me. This meant that I could not open or close the window without help. Sudden rainstorms brought in the rain and nice summer breezes were out of reach for me. It was very frustrating. In our new house we planned windows so that I could reach almost all of them. Now, the breezes come and go as I please!

## Caregiver needs

The importance of supporting your caregiver cannot be underestimated. In fact, my husband and I could write a whole book about it. If you or your loved one have help from a caregiver that does not live with you, you must consider how they will come and go from your house and where they will be situated when then are there. Is it possible for them to come in a separate entrance? If so, it will help maintain some privacy for the rest of the household.

If you need help from someone who spends the night, make space for them to have their own room with a private bathroom or a separate small apartment like a granny flat. If a separate overnight room is not needed, consider the size of the room where your caregiver spends time. Not only will you need transfer space for yourself (in the bedroom and the bathroom), you will need room for someone else to be there to assist. Perhaps you need to allow space for a comfortable chair and a side table for an overnight attendant? If possible, include your caregiver in the discussions about your home plans.

I never did like getting sand in my bathing suit, but I did enjoy walking on the beach. Here you can see the Mobi-Mat at Main Beach in Goderich, on the shore of Lake Huron. We have some of this at our farm, and once we are in less of a muddy state, we'll put some out for access to the larger gardens.

## What do you like to do?

Brainstorm everything you wish you had the space to do and write it down. Once you have made your wish list, prioritize it and start to plan space for it. If you are newly injured and are not sure how much you will recover, set goals for yourself. What do you not currently have space for? Example: storage for your hobbies that you can reach. What sort of setup do you need? Example: a large tabletop that you can roll under or sit at comfortably? Is there an outdoor activity that you miss? Example: maybe you need to install Mobi-Mats to get around on your property or raised beds so you can garden? Perhaps it's woodworking or cooking? Maybe sewing, crafts or outdoor experiences? Remember to include space for exercise equipment that you have or may get in the future. Example: a standing frame that also requires transfer space.

## Safety

When you start to consider all the steps you can take to improve safety, you must think about yourself and your (current or future) caregiver. Falls happen, and usually in the space and time that you least expect it. They will happen in the house, outside, on a ramp, down a slope and because of water on the floor. When I look back at the falls I have had, they have been in the bathroom after a shower (yes, soaking wet), outside after accidentally rolling into the driveway ditch, and the worst? Rolling off the edge of the sidewalk and falling into the campfire.

How do you avoid these traumatic and dangerous events from happening? By planning safe surroundings. Your choice of flooring, level thresholds and outdoor landscaping will make all the difference. When considering flooring, get it wet and check how slippery it is. Find one that has a bit of texture or grit incorporated into the surface. This will help both shoes and wheels from sliding on wet surfaces.

Ask your landscaper to make the land slope gradually away from your house so you don't have to navigate steep surfaces (see the note about slope). If you have a long hallway, consider having a railing – it will help steady you as you go. All grab bars need to be attached to a solid surface (into backing).

Before the build (while we still had grass) I used to try and get around in the yard. Sometimes this happened – mostly in slow motion. *No one was hurt in the making of this book!*

The other problem with falls (aside from injuries) is that you have to get back up. This is where we need to consider the caregiver. Lifting is the most common way that caregivers and support workers end up with injuries (arms, shoulders or back). Whether it is from lifting, assisting with transfers or support to walk down a hall – these situations all put strain on the caregiver and need to be avoided.

I am so thankful that my husband can lift me, but we won't be able to rely on that backup plan forever. There must be a safe way for you to get up after a fall because no matter how much you plan, falls will happen.

Keep reading and you'll find out how this injury happened. What you see is the bottom of the stainless-steel prep sink, and how close it is to the top of my knees. You can also see the bandage on my right knee... I wonder what the connection is?

## Burns

Burns are the kind of accident that happen before you even realize what is going on. The stove top, oven, microwave, barbecue, fire pit and the temperature of your hot water are all possible hazards. Each one needs to be planned for, especially if you have less sensation. When choosing your stove top be sure that the element control dials are along the front or side, so they are close enough for you to reach without having to put your hand and arm over a hot surface or pot. Plan for a wall oven with a side swing door so you don't have to reach very far into the oven to pull out your hot tray or dish. When the plumbing is installed you can choose to have temperature-controlled faucets. This way you can control how hot the water is when it comes out of the taps in the bathroom and kitchen. Ask your plumber to recess, wrap and cover pipes so that hot surfaces do not come in contact with your knees.

---

*ONCE BURNED, TWICE SHY*
*The prep sink in my kitchen ended up being ½*
*inch deeper than the original plan. I waved*
*this off as insignificant even though my knees*
*touched the bottom of the stainless-steel*
*sink. This didn't become an issue until six*
*months after moving in when I strained a pot*
*of boiled potatoes down the sink. I was pulled*
*right in tight to the counter (for safety) and*
*ended up scalding my right knee. I am now*
*on the hunt for a sink the same size, but one*
*inch shallower. The ironic part was that I had*
*just finished editing the above paragraph*
*about the danger of sinks...*

---

## Skin wounds

I have been lucky to not have had any friction or pressure wounds since my SCI. But they happen and usually without your knowledge. As you make your plans to renovate or build, always think about what you will sit on when you are not in your wheelchair. Do you have a chair or couch raised so you can easily transfer in and out? Is your shower bench the right height and does it have a padded surface? Is your toilet the right height, with a backrest (lid or tank) and is the seat tight? (I have had the skin on my leg pinched between the seat and the toilet bowl).

What about getting in and out of your car – is your transferring surface smooth? Is your outdoor furniture well cushioned? Do the cushions get hot when sitting in the sun? Any transfer that causes friction to your skin or any seated or lying position that causes uneven pressure (like leaning on the hard tile surface in the shower) can cause skin breakdown. Pressure sores can develop without you even knowing that they are there. Combined with reduced blood circulation, they can take a very long time to heal. Planning to prevent skin issues is essential.

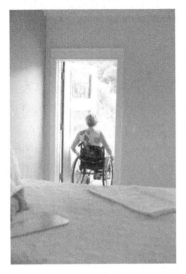

This is what I call my "emergency escape" door. It goes from our bedroom to the back patio. If I need to get out in a hurry because the house is filling with smoke, I can't exactly crawl out the window.

We had a debate about the direction the door should swing, and in the end, it was decided that it should swing out. The porch is covered somewhat here, but we (that's the "royal we") will have to keep the snow cleared away in the winter.

## Emergency and communications

Getting into the house is one thing. It's a completely different matter to get out – especially when you are in a hurry. Plan for it, right from the start. With the hope that you will never need to escape from your home due to fire or carbon monoxide, you still need to have a plan. When you can't crawl out a window, there must be an alternative. Figure out how to have at least two exits, preferably on opposite sides or ends of the house. Emergency exit doors should, ideally, swing out and be cleared of snow in the wintertime. Lay out your escape route so you know what your quickest route out of the house is no matter where you happen to be. If the main route is not possible, which way will you go? Can you get far enough away from the house to be safe if you are on your own? Is there going to be snow blocking your emergency passageway in the wintertime? Will other members of your household (like children) need your assistance? Once you move in, practice your plan.

Fire safety devices are a part of the building code, including smoke and carbon monoxide detectors and fire extinguishers. Their locations should be strategic, and all members of the household should know their location and what they sound and look like. Visual fire alarms are essential for homes where hearing loss is an issue. Make sure you can reach the fire extinguishers!

Communication is a big part of safety. I have been told by many wheelchair users to ALWAYS have my phone with me. But sometimes you put it down and don't have it when you need it most. A landline that connects to the bathroom or bedroom is ideal for emergencies, especially when mobile phones sometimes go "missing". What do you use to communicate when the power goes out? Who are your emergency contacts? Have them posted and programed into your phone under ICE (in case of emergency).

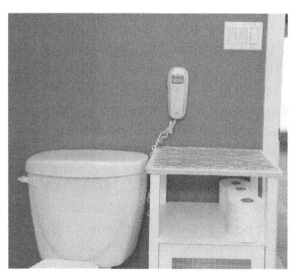

Yes, this is a phone beside a toilet. It belongs to my friend Chris – she's a super smart, hardworking woman who just happens to have a spinal cord injury. I've learned a lot from her and many of our house decisions came from experiences I had while staying at her house.

# Independence

## Bathroom

This is the room where independence and the preservation of dignity are of utmost importance. You must be able to close the door, do your bathroom routine on your own (or with enough space for you and your caregiver) and shower or bathe. If you use a commode or shower chair, your bathroom has to be big enough for it and your wheelchair. Otherwise you will have to push your chair out of the bathroom in order to maneuver in that space. Based on your current situation, what restrictions does your bathroom space put on your independence? List all the key things that you would like to see changed.

## Kitchen

If you like to cook, or want to learn how to cook, then you've got to do it right. Chapter 5 is all about kitchens, but first, consider your overall goals for cooking. Even if you are a "cook from frozen" chef, create roll-under countertop for your prep area. You need knee clearance for the counter and sink and you need to be able to reach the controls and burners on the stove/oven. Even if you do not want to cook, you'll want to be able to make a pot of tea and wash your hands in the kitchen! What does your current kitchen allow you to do well? What do you wish you'd be able to do? What appliances do you plan to have and how much reach do you need to have to use them effectively and safely?

## Raising Children

If you have a young family and use a mobility device, you are going to have to consider turning radius in all of your rooms. Getting into your child's bedroom, navigating the stuffies, clothes and Nerf blasters on the floor and getting out again is tough for anyone, let alone when wheels are involved. Plan to make modifications to the height of the change table, dresser, closet rods and shelves, crib and bookshelves – and remember, if you can reach it, they can too!

This is the endless pool we built to be able to swim indoors, all four seasons. It is my very favourite place in the whole house. Freedom. But I'm not the only one who likes it.

*My kids*

When we moved into this house, I was so excited for my kids' (ages 13 and 16) bedrooms on the main floor. I would be able to tuck them in and kiss them goodnight! Well, the best laid plans – of course, I can barely get into their rooms, let alone to their beds!

I have had to "snowplow" to get to my daughter's desk so I could retrieve my tweezers! (There's an invention in there somewhere!) As we set up more shelving and storage, I'm hopeful this will improve.

## From the outdoors in and back again

Whether you are arriving in your car or coming in from the sidewalk you need to be able to do it in all seasons. You'll want to come in through the door with a bag on your lap – and keep it there. Ask your contractor to consider the slope of your ramp (if you need one – see Chapter 5 – A word about slope) and help you identify ways to protect your entry from weather. A covered porch will help reduce how wet you get while you unlock your door and may reduce the need to shovel snow – who wants to shovel? Also, be sure to insist that door frames are sunk into the foundation to reduce the bump at the threshold. You want to have as smooth an entry as possible.

## Other equipment

Your outdoor chair, patio set, bike, ping pong table or golf clubs – whatever you have that gets you out of the house – you need to be able to get at it! Having space to store it is fantastic, but not if someone else needs to get it out every time you want to use it.

What you see here are my two other sets of wheels: my handbike and my Mountain Trike.

This requires advanced planning and if you forget, you are out of luck until assistance arrives. You will also need space to transfer safely. List the equipment, tools or supplies you'd like to be able to get to.

## Convenience requires creativity

Most of what I talk about in this book are things I consider as "needs", but you also have to consider your "wants". These are the extras, the things on your wish list. Whether it means reaching your scrapbooking case or storing your ATV, let your "wants" be known! Tell your architect, designer and builder what your wishes are. Think big and be creative! Fold down desktops for your hobbies work well and storage below a bench with pull out drawers is very space efficient. Create a drop zone for keys and mail in the hall and one for food beside the fridge. Tiny House building guides are a great way to get creative ideas because of their ingenious ways to make space "appear".

This is an IKEA shelf turned sideways. Towel are easy to reach and to put away.

## Think to the future

No matter your age, you have a future. You don't know where you will end up – or what you will be able to do; it may be more, it may be less, so be prepared for both.

### Growing

Young kids grow into older, bigger, heavier kids. Carrying your young person around may not be an option forever. Solutions for stairs, transfers to vehicles and into the tub need to grow with your child. Adults grow too – just not in the way we all wish to. We get heavier, even when we try hard not to. Just like for kids, we need to plan for that. Electrical outlets in the ceiling of the bedroom and bathroom are an example of preparing for future lift installations. What will you need more help with: entryway, stairs, bathtub, vehicle transfers, carrying groceries...?

## STEVEN'S HOUSE

*Two months after we moved in, a local family came to see our house. They were trying to decide whether to build new or renovate their farmhouse. Their son Steven is now a teenager, and because of his genetic condition, he is not able to walk on his own. Both parents have overuse injuries to their arms; they wanted help figuring out how to help Steven get around the house with less physical stress. After we sat at the kitchen table and looked at the layout of their current home, we went over to our old house (which was still standing). I gave them a few minutes to look around and see how I had made do with so many obstacles. Finally, Steven's mother said to me "Wow. You get it. You really get it." What she meant was that I wasn't just a wheelchair user with a fabulously accessible new home, I was someone who had lived in a less than ideal situation but had made it work. So will they.*

## Recovery

If you have sustained an injury (like an SCI) and are making plans to come home from Rehab, your recovery is just beginning. You have no idea how far you will come and what you will be capable of, so plan for the best. Plan for your dreams. Perhaps you are young? Will you be living with your family forever? What do you want for your own space? Do you have space for privacy or for your future partner? (See Wheel Pad in Chapter 6 for ideas)

Give yourself space for stretching and exercise.
My favourite place for physio is in the pool!

## Aging

It's inevitable. Complications will arise due to illness, falls, reduced strength and so many other unknown factors. Because of this, make sure that construction or renovations are done to include backing in walls for future grab bars, lifts, and plumbing. As you build, you can plan to move your laundry from the basement to the main floor or change a formal dining room into your master bedroom (a great idea). It's possible to frame for it now (like a 36" doorway to the bathroom) and expose the opening later when you need it. Build slab-on-grade with no basement to reduce maintenance and cleaning.

## Chapter 3: Summary

- ❏ Identify your personal needs first, such as space for a mobility device and caregiver.
- ❏ What are your potential safety risks?
- ❏ How can you maximize independence?
- ❏ How will you deal with emergencies?
- ❏ What do you need to be as independent as possible?
- ❏ Future considerations like growth and aging must be considered.

# Tweaking "regular" house decisions increases comfort

## Windows

MANY OLDER HOMES have windows that are too high for someone who is seated. Depending on how your house is situated (i.e. you won't want to look into your neighbour's windows), you'll want to have windows that are as big as you can afford. Window ledges that are low (even as low as 27" from the floor) allow you to see outside from a seated position as well as letting in lots of light. They can also be a surface where you can put your morning cup of coffee while you watch the sun rise. Cats and books also tend to find a home on a window ledge!

These are the crank style windows we chose to install. They have one lock, which means I can reach to open, lock and unlock.

Windows that crank open (called casement) rather than double hung, are going to be easier for you to operate. Casement windows are now usually made with only one lock, rather than two. Be sure to ask for a crank on the bottom ledge and the lock located within your reach.

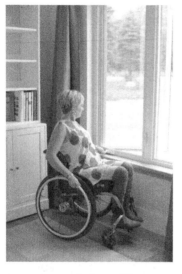

Window height is key to comfort, too. In the old house I was only able to see out the front windows; now I can see out every which way!

Think ahead about window coverings – you may want to reduce direct sunlight in your home. TV rooms should be able to be darkened and it is also nice to sleep in the dark! Closing curtains or shades will also help maintain reasonable summer temperatures. All window coverings need to be easy to open and close. There are several ways to do this. Lightweight curtains with grommets slide easily along a rod. Heavier curtains can have long, solid, pulls (called drapery batons). If you prefer the look of a blind, just extend the length of the pull so it can be reached from a seated position. Once you're in your house, be sure to keep furniture out of the way and stuff off the floor so you can reach all your windows.

## Temperature control

"Normal" room temperature is 20°C. Thermostats are usually set between 18°C and 23°C, depending on the season. Most people don't realize how important it is to keep a room at, or near, room temperature. It affects your mood, ability to focus, fatigue and the amount of tension in your shoulders and back. Temperature is especially significant for those with nervous system conditions like spinal cord injuries or MS. When unable to regulate temperature (through sweating or shivering) properly, the temperature of the environment needs to be carefully controlled.

---

## MY NON-WORKING PERSONAL THERMOSTAT

*My first summer at home after my injury was a pretty steep learning curve, especially when it came to regulating temperature. I learned that not only does my body not sweat, I can't tell when I'm hot! I was out in the yard with my family on a warm (not hot) day. After a while, I figured that I'd had enough sun and I should go inside. What I didn't realize was that I was seriously overheating, and by the time we got inside I was feeling sick and claustrophobic. It took over an hour of lying in a cool room before I began to feel better.*

---

Do your research. There are many different heating and cooling systems to choose from; find out which ones suit the set up of your home and go from there. By far the most consistent level of heat comes from the floor. In-floor heating involves heat being released from either electrical coils or water heated by a boiler piped through the cement floor. The only air movement will be from the air exchanger, which means in the winter there is no air blowing from vents which tend to create drafts. In-floor heat provides a very consistent level of heat, and sound (from a furnace) is reduced to almost nothing.

In the summertime you do want air to move! It's one thing to carry a spray bottle full of water around to mimic the effect of sweat, but it's even better if you cool your house properly. An AC system installed so that cool air falls from above is more efficient than having it blow up from floor vents. Adjust vents so they do not blow on your body directly.

If you have floor vents, be sure they have a heavy-duty cover that is firmly secured to the floor. I have cracked several plastic vent covers in other people's homes: "Oh, by the way, I cracked your vent cover while I was in the bathroom... sorry."

Ask your heating/cooling specialists to mount the controls no higher than 42" from the floor. Ideally you will be operating this system on your own, so you need to be able to see the control screen and make the necessary adjustments.

---

### ELEVATORS
*Because we build slab-on-grade with no second storey, we had no need for any kind of elevator or lift. I have tried out quite a few at different people's homes, some that were home-made and others that were proper elevators with call buttons and sound notifications. The expense of an elevator is something that we wanted to avoid, not just the initial cost, but also the cost of regular maintenance and service calls. By all means, if you have a second level, install an elevator, but do your research to make sure you get the device that will work best for you. Service calls because you are stuck in between floors can be an inconvenience and expensive...*

---

## Flooring

Your choice of flooring will be one of the most important decisions you make. Especially if you use a wheelchair. Options are endless but the best way to make your decision is to try it out.

Put the samples on the floor and roll or walk over them – look from all angles to see what marks are left behind and how easily it scratches. Ask about durability, water resistance, warranty, general wear and tear. The more shine on the floor and the darker the colour the more you will see your tire marks.

This is tile! Vinyl plank tile to be precise. We waffled a bit about doing this pattern set into the darker grey, as we'll have to like it for a long time – but I'm so glad we did, because we love it!
The floors are heated (in-floor heat with a Geo-thermal heat source) so in winter, snow melt from boots dries up quickly.

It's one thing to take off your shoes; it's entirely another to re-move your wheels! Unless you have someone to clean your tires every time you come into the house there is always going to be dirt and dust tracked in. Make sure you choose something that will show less. For us, it seemed impossible to find something that showed no marks. Testing everything we could find helped and bringing it home to see it in actual sunlight allowed us to see the end result. If possible, wet the flooring and see how slippery it is. Again, the more sheen, the more likely your wheels will slide when wet. Be aware that some types of vinyl actually have cushion in them which makes rolling a mobility device more like rolling on a beach. There are great ways to make your flooring more inter-esting, like using a pattern or variations on colour themes throughout the house or in areas that you want to accent.

Carpets of any kind, for lack of a better work, suck. Stay away from them. Wall-to-wall carpet is laid with under pad and to-gether they will seriously slow you down while they suck up your energy. Even short pile area rugs cause problems by creating trip hazards. Just say "no" to carpets.

## Electrical considerations

Plan for light switches beside your bed (at a height you're able to reach while lying down) and in multiple locations around all the rooms and doorways in the house. Install them six inches lower than regular height (41" from the floor) and choose switches that are large, as they require less dexterity and accuracy (I'm sometimes moving fast when I pass by a light switch). Switches and outlets should also be placed along counters where they can be reached at the side or along the front of the counter. This eliminates the need for reaching over a counter to turn lights off or on. Place pot lights or task lighting where you will be spending time. Some pot lights can even be turned to point in a specific direction.

Place outlets in locations where you know you'll need them for equipment, AV, and at the front and/or side of countertops in the kitchen and bathroom. If you have a kitchen island, run power up the middle so you can have outlets or a charging station on either end. In the bathroom, install outlets beside the toilet, in the ceiling for future equipment and beside the bathroom sink – not at the back of the counter. This will give you easy access for your hair dryer now and any future equipment needs – there is such a thing as a toilet seat lift! Outlets can be raised to be 20" off the finished floor.

The final accessibility-related electrical considerations are the height, location and direction of the electrical panel. Ideally you will have the panel placed horizontally in a room where you can get to it, located between 43" and 47" off the floor.

## Doors and doorways

The ideal door width is 38" as almost any mobility device (or couch) will fit through it. However, it may mean ordering custom doors. The door width you choose can also depend on where that door leads. Front door and garage entries should be wide. Consider also making your bathroom doorway 38", especially if you use a shower chair. For safety reasons, bathroom doors should open out in case someone or something falls behind the door.

This is the electrical panel in the garage. It was Wayne's idea to turn it sideways – it still meets code requirements, and I can reach it!
The page in the plastic sleeve on the left outlines the switch numbers and their locations.

Wider doors obviously accommodate larger mobility devices, but they also allow you to be less specific with your travel! Running into a door frame that is brand new and has been freshly painted does not feel good! Exterior door frames should be sunk into the foundation of the home; this way door jams will be lower and closer to level, creating less of a threshold in the entryway.

Lever door handles can be operated with a closed fist; door-knobs not so easily! Lever handles are a true example of Universal Design – everyone benefits; even a foot can open a door while your hands are full of groceries. Doors that swing out should have a D-handle on the inside, hinge side of the door. That way you don't have to turn around or back track to pull the door closed behind you. Automatic closers with the right amount of pressure on the springs are also great, and sometimes necessary for Building Code Compliance (like for the garage).

*ACCESSIBLE BY ACCIDENT*
*Sometimes neat things happen by accident. When we choose our door styles, we went with three panel Shaker-style interior doors because we liked the look. What surprised me was that the lower centre panel acts like a handle I can use to pull doors closed. No need to put a D-pull on the hinge side of the door! The other door-related trick I use is the frame. The trim we choose is ¾" deep which is just enough for me to grab onto when I whip around a corner into a room.*

*You will encounter different options when it comes to locking your exterior and interior doors. Locks built into the handle can be either pushed or turned. Choose the push button lock as it requires less manual dexterity than the turn button. Locks for privacy in the bathroom are important, but be sure the option you choose can be opened from the*

If you choose to have a solid front door, be sure to install a peep-
hole at the height of the person who will be using it. You can

also put in more than one! Another way to know who is at your door is to have windows within the door. They are a great way to let in light, see outside, and know who is approaching the house.

## General storage

There is a lot of planning (and sorting) that needs to happen in order to accommodate your "stuff". Consider the "less is more" option as you plan your storage spaces. What I mean is, get rid of your stuff, so you don't have to store it! If you have no base-ment, then storage within the rooms and hallways of the house becomes prime real estate! Be sure to ask your designer to in-corporate storage into your architectural drawings. Use up every nook and cranny of spare space.

Once you are in your new home, organize for ease of access. What things do you use most? They (like towels and toilet pa-per) should be placed on lower shelves and at the front. Off-season clothing and duvets can be put away in containers or boxes on higher, out-of-the-way places like in the top of closets.

Be sure to organize so you reduce shoulder strain and be cautious of how heavy things are on upper shelves. Shelving that is not deep allows you to see everything at once, so you can find what you need quickly. Place shelving at height intervals where your goods fit. In deep closet spaces and when possible, have drawers instead of cupboards – drawers are so much more accessible for everyone.

Yes! Glasses in a drawer!

## It's the little things

Stay in the loop while decisions are being made, and while the work is being done. If you can't access the worksite, get someone to take video or photos for you to review so you can have input. Have that friend take measurements so you know elevations of counters, heights of switches and controls. Mistakes can be made and the earlier you catch it, the less it will cost to fix. It only takes two inches for your toilet to be too far from the wall. This creates a domino effect of the grab bar not being close enough for easy transfers and can lead to the potential for shoulder injury. It's going to be hard, but it is so important to stay on top of each stage of construction.

## Chapter 4: Summary

- ❏ Choose the windows that will maximize light and the view.
- ❏ Heating and cooling the house is more important than you think.
- ❏ Flooring choices are not just for looks.
- ❏ Changes to electrical layout save personal energy consumption.
- ❏ Doors, doorways and handles allow for safety and ease of use.
- ❏ Storage cannot be forgotten!

# Room by room

## The Bathroom

WHERE YOU WISH you didn't have to spend a lot of time, but you do, so let's make yours awesome.

### Bathtub or Shower?

Choosing tub vs shower is a matter of personal preference. If you are able to lower yourself into the tub and get back out, that's fantastic! Some people have a bathtub and a roll-in shower, or a walk-in tub with a door and a seat. If transferring is not your thing or you need a lift to do so, a roll-in shower with a commode is likely your best bet.

Zero threshold is the true roll-in shower. There should be no height transition between the floor in your bathroom and the floor of the shower. There may be a change in flooring (from vinyl to ceramic tile, for example) but it must all be flush with only caulking or grout in between. Avoid using a rubber lip or edge that you have to get over. Not only are they in the way of a smooth transition, they are a tripping hazard. The rubber also breaks down over time and will be difficult to replace and keep sealed.

The floor in the shower must be sloped toward the drain. A channel drain at the front of the shower (rather than a circle drain) will allow the slope to be gradual (mine is 2.5%) and all in one direction. Using a circle drain in the centre of the floor means that the floor has to be sloped in many directions. This can cause a wheeled device to lose traction or the user to become off balance. Talk to your contractor about how to allow for drainage and safety at the same time.

Look for: shower wand that swivels and moves up and down plus a "rain shower" for the taller users; channel drain at the front of the shower; soap dispenser with several hooks; grab bar with a small towel to keep my chair dry after I shower; shower bench that folds up and out of the way; reacher (hanging on towel bar) and hook for a towel.

We goofed again with heights; Theo has to duck under the curtain rod!

If using a shower curtain, mount the rod so the curtain it is not touching the floor. You don't want to catch it under your wheels and pull the whole thing down on top of you. You can also prevent this from happening if you use a rod that is securely attached to the wall, rather than one that is spring loaded. Shower curtains are a great way to protect your wheelchair from getting wet while you shower. If you transfer to a shower bench, you can push your chair just far enough so the curtain can keep it dry and you can reach it when you are done. It's also a good idea to have a reacher in the shower. Sometimes your wheels go a bit too far and that wash cloth or razor can sometimes get away!

The type of seat and location of grab bars in the shower are also a matter of personal preference. Again, practice how you will be seated and where you need to place your hands for balance or leverage. You can use the option of a tub with a shower bench across it, but it's not always practical. Lifting legs over the edge of the tub can be energy consuming or difficult if you have muscle spasticity. A shower with a bench or a rolling commode improves the safety aspect of bathing. If skin damage or pressure sores are a potential issue for you, choose a bench that is padded rather than just solid wood or plastic. This will reduce pressure on your buttocks and legs and allow you to sit for as long as you like! Install a soap dispenser in your shower. This frees up your other hand to use for balance and means you are not jugging bottles of products. A towel bar for a face cloth and a couple of low hooks for your towel just outside the shower will also be useful.

Be specific about the height of your shower controls and the temperature of the hot water. You need to be able to adjust everything with one hand from a seated position (i.e. on your shower bench). The hand shower should slide easily on the wall bar and have a flexible hose. Test how easily it slides on the bar (should be able to do it with one hand) before you buy it and be there when your plumber is deciding where to locate it. It has to be within reach of where you will be seated!

---

### "IT'S ACCESSIBLE"

*It is always very obvious to me that the people who design and install "accessible" showers at hotels are not the ones who are going to be seated while taking a shower. The classic (not) accessible hotel shower is one that has a seat at the rear of the shower and the controls at the front. In this situation (when I'm on my own) I think "I can always shower when I get home... sigh."*

---

## The sink etc.

With each sink that you install, be sure you can roll under it without hitting your knees. It should have a rear drain and covered or wrapped pipes. Choose a spout that extends out into the bowl of the sink rather than just to the position of the drain. This means you don't have to reach quite so far to wash your hands and brush your teeth. Lever taps are universal, and they allow for better temperature control.

The bathroom sink is a bit different than your kitchen sink because in the bathroom you'll want to get your chin right over the edge for teeth brushing. Do some accurate measuring for knee clearance and have the sink installed as close to the front edge of the counter as possible. The height should also be comfortable for resting your elbows on while you wash your face, shave or dry your hair.

If wall space above your sink is limited, try a mirror that tilts. This allows the tall and the not tall to have a look at themselves. Before you install the mirror, make sure you are able to reach it. If you have the space, a bigger mirror is better because it will also help your bathroom feel more spacious.

Choose a counter height that will work best for you (between 32" and 36" is common). Two different counter heights can also work if you have space. Think about side-to-side reach and balance before you decide on the width of your counter and where drawers should go. Ideally, you want to be able to get to everything you need without having to move your wheels. You will need to consider a space for a hand towel and face cloth, your hair dryer (which can hang to the side under the sink), toothbrush, makeup, towel storage, etc.

Lights should be placed above the shower, sink and toilet with task lighting controls within easy reach beside the sink.

## Toilet and transfers

Even if you are not using a toilet "the traditional way" right now, you may progress to the point where you are able to. Make sure you choose one that will work for you down the road. You'll want it to be high. A tall bowl means easier transfers if you use a wheelchair, and it also means less leg work if you are standing. Universal height of a toilet is 18" or higher. Of course, if you have shorter legs, you'll pick what works best for you. Choose a bowl that is oblong and a toilet seat that has a front opening. This will allow you to get your hand between your legs whether you stand or not.

Make sure you have either a tank or a toilet seat lid. This will improve the safety of the skin on your back and will help with balance. There a few different ways to hang a toilet roll; some grab bars even include a space for toilet paper. Make sure that it is hung below the grab bar, out of the way of your knee transfer space but still within reach (6" from the front edge of the toilet bowl).

Ideally, you want to have something for leverage and balance on both sides of the toilet. Some people don't like the look of grab bars, so they use a ledge or small shelf instead. Use whatever is most practical for you! Height is important (between 29

½" and 33 ½" is universal) but do what is best for your situation. An L-bar works for those who can stand: the horizontal for side-to-side leverage and the vertical bar for pulling up. If you don't have the option of attaching a grab bar to both sides of the toilet then consider a "drop-down" bar. This bar gives you the versatility of having a bar to lean on, plus it can be moved out of the way for transfers. There are different kinds of movable bars, some that swing down and some that swing out.

Custom made storage cubbies hide my supplies in this half-wall beside the toilet. It is also a ledge for a cup of coffee or your latest reading materials.

### Bathroom storage

Many people need to store more than just toilet paper near the toilet, so consider shelving or small drawers that you can reach while seated. You'll need to get creative! Use the space between studs or install a small wall-mounted cabinet. Storage behind the toilet is not ideal as it is difficult to turn your body, balance and reach all at the same time. Having supplies in view also gives you peace of mind — is it time to reorder catheters? It's also a good idea to have a shelf or ledge to put things on (like your phone or your morning cup of coffee).

For garbage, some people use a plastic bag hanging from a grab bar, some have a garbage with a lid. Consider what space you have available and make sure you can move it easily and empty it yourself.

Hang towels on bars placed within reach (39" off the floor) or use low profile hooks. Use open shelves or drawers for clean towels rolled up and at an accessible height.

Do you have a commode that you need space for? You can store it in the shower, but then others will have to move it out of the way when they shower. Plan a designated parking space for your shower wheels to be.

Everyone likes to be warm in the shower so consider how you can bring more heat to the bathroom, especially if you are renovating an old house. Do you need additional heat for comfort? How can it be accomplished safely and efficiently? Think about adding in-floor heat or maybe a heat lamp in the ceiling. These are the questions to ask your local building store or your contractor – which solution will work best for the space that you have?

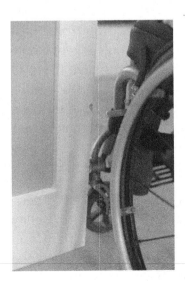

*CORNERS*
*Even if you have a large bathroom, limit the number of sharp corners that you might run into. Tight turning spaces can mean that toes (especially naked ones) can get caught. Even if it's not your toes, it could be your front wheels or foot plate that scrape or dent the corners.*

## Kitchen

Your kitchen will be both beautiful and functional, especially when you consider all of the following ideas. Build this space to feed your soul.

### Countertops

Start by deciding where your counter will go and what the depth will be. Measure your reach from two different positions. First, pull up under the counter and reach ahead – how far ahead can you reach? Next, pull up beside the counter (side saddle) and reach to the side and measure that. You want to be able to reach to the back of the counter with a cloth in your hand.

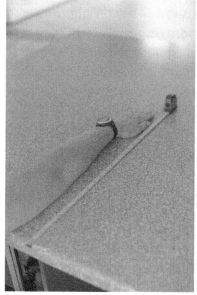

This is my reach when I'm side saddle. I can get just to the middle of the island!

Standard counter depth is 24" but ask your kitchen planner to do what works for you. Universal Design in kitchens often recommends a pull-out work surface (see Drop Zone next page). The problem with a pull-out is once you have it pulled out, with food and a cutting board on it, you have to move everything to push that surface back in and out of the way. Use pull-outs for counter space only if you don't have enough room to make roll-under counters.

You get to choose YOUR counter height! As you make this decision, think about the future. Kids will grow (and their mobility devices will get larger) and you may need to transition from standing to a seated position, so plan for it. Measure your knee clearance and ideal work height (32" to 37"). Something that I did not consider when planning my knee clearance is that in the future, my wheelchair height may change. If you use a lapboard while working in the kitchen, add height to your knees so it fits under the counter too.

Here you can see the lovely rounded surface of the bullnose counter edge. All the counter surfaces in the house are the same material, colour and finish.

After you have decided on the look of your counter, you'll need to choose the material it's made from. Transferring heavy, hot pots from stove to sink can be a challenge. Sliding hot things across a counter is only possible if it is heat proof. You should also reduce the distance that a pot of pasta has to travel between the cooktop and the sink. When choosing a counter profile (edge) find one that is "forearm friendly" (i.e. rounded). I have reduced core strength and therefore need to lean on the edge of whatever surface I am sitting at. Leaning on an edge that is 90° is hard on the forearms. The profile on our counter is "full bullnose" which is a very comfortable edge.

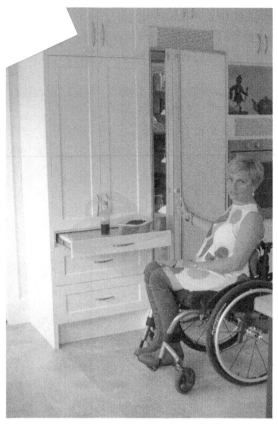

## Have you got a "drop zone"?

Whether it is beside your fridge, under your wall oven or in front of your microwave, a drop zone is for both safety and convenience. I use this space to place items as I take them in and out of the fridge. It saves multiple trips and energy. Although my drop zone can often become the "kids are late for school sandwich making station," ideally, your drop zone is not a work surface, just a temporary place to put things. If it does become a work surface, then you have to put everything away before you can slide it back and out of your way.

### Sinks

Just as you did for your bathroom, consider sink and pipe insulation, rear position of the drain and the type of levers for your taps. One hand operation for the taps is best, but individual hot and cold levers can mean more accurate temperature control. Add a spray nozzle with a flexible hose on the side of the tap – it can also work as a pot filler. If you choose to go with a stainless-steel sink, remember that the heat will transfer more readily through metal and can come in contact with your legs

underneath. Be sure you have enough clearance, so your skin won't be in contact, or, that your sink base and pipes are insulated to protect your legs. Double sinks are helpful but do test your reach side to side and make sure you can access the draining rack.

*WET SLEEVES*
*One thing I would change about my new kitchen is the height of the dish-washing sink. I don't particularly love the feeling of water running down to my elbows and into my sleeves! Be sure your sink is at a height that works for you – mine just needs to be one inch lower. Now I wash dishes with a towel along the front edge of the sink which solves the problem.*

If you have space for a second sink, install a prep sink the size of a small bar sink. It will come in handy for washing your hands (or fruits and vegetables) while preparing a meal. A small, low sink close by keeps messy hands off your wheels or walker. A small counter space between the sink and the stove is also something to consider as it allows you to prepare food, wash your hands and reach the cooktop without having to move.

## Appliances

The universal height of a dishwasher base is actually 18" off the floor! This height means that tall people and people in a seated position can reach into the dishwasher with ease. A higher dishwasher will raise the counter height where the dishwasher is located, so be sure that this works in your plan before you decide to do it. There are

also dishwasher drawers that wash smaller loads and are easier to reach because they pull out.

Although they are hard to come by, a wall oven with a side hinge opening door (or French doors) is really helpful. Traditional ovens require you to reach and lean into the oven to remove hot food. Side swing doors allow you to pull the hot dish toward you without leaning in. Mount the wall oven so that the door swings

over top of your knees; this makes cooking and baking even easier.

Whether you have a stove or a separate cooktop and oven, the controls must be front or side mounted. Controls that are on the back of the cooktop require you to reach over top of a hot surface. Even if you use your long wooden spoon to push the buttons, there is potential for burns from steaming pots.

Your choice of heat source is personal (I love cooking with gas), but induction cooking is the safest as it stays cool to the touch. If you have the space for a separate cooktop and oven, be sure to mount the cooktop at a height where you can roll under without the lower surface coming in contact with your legs. Look at the specs of your choices so you know the depth of the surface. In your plan, leave at least a 1" gap between your knees and the lower surface so  they don't come in contact. The best part of having a lower cooktop is the fact that I can see inside the pot that I am stirring!

If you choose a stove (oven and cooktop combined) make sure the controls are within reach and that you can see the picture for each dial. It's easy to turn the wrong burner on by accident – and quite dangerous! When opening the oven, reaching over the door and inside for heavy items will be tricky, which is why a side swing door is so helpful. You don't realize the trunk strength that is required until you don't have it! Try out the handle on the oven door before you purchase the appliance. Be sure you can get a firm grasp on it.

Our microwave is located under the counter; the base of it is at 21". It works for all of us, even though Theo grumbles about having to reach so far down.

From an accessibility perspective, reach is the biggest consideration for choosing your fridge and freezer. Visit your local appliance store and try out every fridge, freezer and combination that they have. Can you easily open the door? How many shelves can you reach? How far back can you reach? Are the shelves and door storage adjustable? Is there a light? Are the drawers large enough to hold all your produce?

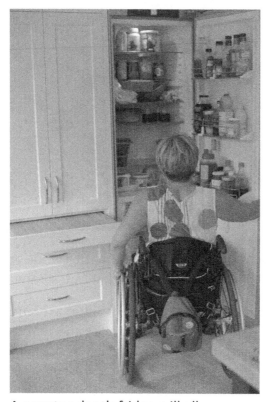

This is a European-style counter-depth fridge. There are three produce drawers with "ever fresh" that keeps the produce fresher, longer. I can't reach everything on the top shelves, but with enough training, the rest of the household is learning to put the things I don't use up there.

I can reach right to the back of the fridge. The drawers are lightweight and make it easy to find what I am looking for.

We have a full upright freezer in the pantry.

A counter-depth fridge will allow someone in a seated position to reach almost to the back (so you can reach last week's leftovers). A freezer-on-top means reaching only some of your frozen foods. A freezer at the bottom will take away fridge space. It's a pretty tough decision, which makes trying out as many as possible essential. A separate fridge and freezer are the ultimate if you can make that work. Avoid chest freezers; once you get past the first layer it's tough to reach what you want. Be sure to choose frost-free options – this will save you the time and effort of defrosting.

## Storage and the perks of a pantry

A place for everything... and everything in its place, right? When planning your kitchen layout, consider drawers instead of doors whenever possible. Kitchen cabinet space is always at a premium – I know I have too many mixing bowls and small appliances! Drawers are the answer for everyone – truly Universal Design. Place two or three drawers in a space where you would have had a lower cabinet with two doors. Drawers allow you to pull out what you are looking for, which makes it closer to you and easier to reach. There are lots of ways to organize drawers depending on their depth; square storage containers and square dishes maximize space.

I call it my "party pantry" because it really is quite big. I can open the freezer door and still have room to get around. Eliminating the upper cabinets in a kitchen means you need to find space for everything. That's what the pantry is for!

A Lazy Susan in a corner makes good use of often wasted space. If using one, design it with the cupboard door incorporated into the spinning shelf rather than pull-out. If the door has to be pulled out, then that is one more action you have to take before you can get what you need, plus you have to move around the door.

If you eliminate upper cabinets (because not everyone can reach them), you lose a lot of storage. Make up for this loss by incorporating a pantry into your kitchen plans. It may be one pull-out section, or it may be a whole room, but it's worth whatever space you can manage. Everyone wins when you have a pantry. Using shelving that is not deep (~8") allows you to see what is on the shelf and you don't have to search behind items like you would in a deep cupboard. Small appliances fit nicely on pantry shelves too. Use clear plastic bins for appliances with small parts (i.e. Magic Bullet, blades, base and cups).

If you don't have room for a pantry and have space for upper cabinets, refer to your measurements of reach and know what height will work for you. Pulldown shelving in upper cabinets can also be added so everything is within reach (See Chapter 6 Condo Renovation).

Most everyone keeps their dishes in the upper cabinets. What do you do then, when you eliminate that space? We put all our dishes into drawers, even glasses and mugs. The dish drawer is across from the dishwasher, making unloading as easy as possible. Because of our high ceilings, we have one set of upper cabinets above the fridge. This is where our "good" dishes and serving plates are stored. I'm not concerned about accessing them because I only eat on them when we have company! Mixing bowls and heavy items should go on a shelf that is close to your knee height. Then you can slide it onto your lap board without bending down or reaching up.

The less you move around the kitchen, the less energy you have to expend. Plan to have everything you need right at your cooktop. Hang the fry pan below, place a utensil container on top, and the salt, pepper, butter and oil right beside. Then all you need to do is get the eggs from the fridge and you are ready to cook!

# Bedroom

*Sleeping space*

Obviously, the size of your bed will determine what else you have room for, and that includes you! Think about transfer space and turning radius when you lay out your bedroom. If you are buying a new bed, take into consideration the height of the mattress. You will be transferring to and from your bed many times a day, so it needs to be easy. Visit the store and explain the need for exact height. Give them the measurement you want and see how they can make it happen. It may require different legs or a smaller box spring or base unit. You can have the support of a hospital bed (without having one) by getting an adjustable bed – a great way to prop up your head or your feet as needed. This becomes an important consideration if edema (swelling) is something that happens to your legs/feet.

Place light switches beside the bed so you can turn the lights off after you crawl into bed. Outlets should also go where you think you will need equipment plugged in. An extra plug should always be available beside your bed for charging your device (phone, powerchair, etc.) while you sleep.

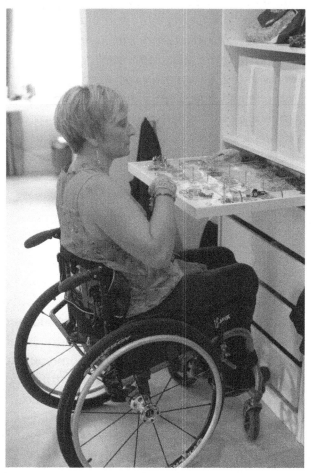

*Closet space*

When organizing your clothing and footwear, hanging rods, drawers and shelves all have their role, so long as you can reach it all. Pull out drawers (on rollers and a track) allow you to get the shirt you want without the rest of them falling down on top of you. You don't want clothing choice to become a physio exercise! Hanging rods can be located at different heights for shirts and dresses or suits. Because my husband is tall, his shirts hang on a rod in the top of the closet and mine hang on the rod below. You can also install rods that pull down – this takes advantage of all your closet space.

There are many ways to incorporate storage around your home.

Baskets and open shelves work well for towels; bed linens can be placed on a shelf in your closet. Off-season items like winter coats can be stuffed in a bin, labeled and put away in a closet for later. Pull-out drawers under a bench or window seat are a great out-of-the-way storage space.

Keep on top of your laundry by having one easy-to-access hamper right where you take off your clothes. That may be in your bathroom, closet or right beside your bed. I have a number of hooks in easy-to-reach places in the bedroom and closet where I hang sweaters and other items that I wear often and aren't ready for the laundry.

## Kids' rooms

When we planned to have no second floor, I thought that the kids (and their bedrooms) would be easy to access! How wrong was I! For three years I had not been in their bedrooms – only the occasional picture to prove that their rooms were in fact "tidy". We made their rooms big enough for their bed and some storage with enough turning radius for my wheelchair. What I did not think about was that even though the room was big enough and the furniture would be out of the way, the clothes and toys on the floor still made their space hard to navigate! A morning wakeup with an opening of their curtains is still impossible without a snowplow attached to the front of my wheelchair! If you have small children, remember to plan for turning radius, crib and change table height and all the stuff that will end up on the floor!

A rare day when I can get to Ella's closet! Another example of pull-out drawers, this time used for shoes and boots.

78

# Coming and going

*From the outside in*

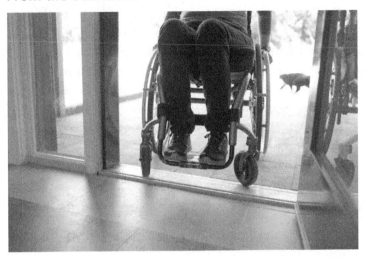

Getting outside is going to help you feel better, so go out there as often as you can. What do you want to do outside? Read, garden, play in the mud? All options are available; you just have to make it work. You can build raised beds for flowers, herbs and vegetables with wood, stone or recycled plastic. Build a bench at transfer height where you can roll onto the grass and lie in the sun. You should also make space under a tree for a quiet mindfulness spot in the shade. Install a fire pit or outdoor fireplace for family and friends to gather around. Your home will be the most accessible place you know, so make it one where you can entertain indoors and out for as many seasons as possible.

Your outdoor space can be as simple or complex as you want and can afford! The most complicated part of landscaping is channeling rain and snowmelt away from your home without creating too much slope. Choose paving stones, concrete or asphalt to create flat surfaces like your patio and front walk. The front walk should come right to the lip of your door with less than ¼" of height difference into your front entrance!

When planning a patio or deck space, keep the same ideas in mind as you have for inside your home. You need access space, turning radius and a smooth surface. There is nothing worse than falling off the edge of the deck or patio – I have done it several times. One fall caused me to land in the fire pit. Protect yourself with deck edge-guards or make your solid surfaces flush with the lawn – that way you can't go over the edge. If possible, roll or walk on your choice of patio stone to make sure that it is smooth enough to not give you trouble (i.e. spasms). If you have a deck that is high enough to need a rail, make sure it's not in your line of sight. Plexiglass is a great material for a railing if you have a view to see.

## Access

Think about how you will access your property and your house. Whether you go out in your wheelchair, scooter or in your car, you need to be able to do it on your own. That means flat solid surfaces (that are easy to clean off in the wintertime).

*A WORD ABOUT SLOPE*
*No matter if it is a driveway, parking lot, street or sidewalk, slope is critical. The steeper the slope, the greater the risk when descending and the more difficult it is to go up. Even code minimum (1:12 or 8.3%) is difficult to navigate. What does 1:12 mean? It means that for every <u>one</u> inch of height (rise) you need your ramp to run 12" horizontally (run). Less slope, 1:15 (6.6%) is better and 1:20 (5.0%) is best. Cross slope (slope running perpendicular to the run) also needs to be considered for drainage purposes on all exterior surfaces (2% max).*

## Ramps

If you need a ramp, then you really need to know your numbers. The less slope, the better (see note about slope). This may mean making your ramp longer than you originally thought it would be. In order to do so, you can make a landing as a "rest" spot on your way up. Consider wrapping your ramp around a corner if necessary, in order for it to be manageable. Talk to your designer about how you can incorporate the ramp into the look of the house – ramps don't have to be ugly!

Building a walled flower bed and matching the materials to the exterior of your home can make it seamless. As you plan, think about snow removal because you will need space between the ramp and the railing to push snow through. Also remember to look up and see what is going to be overtop of your ramp; you don't want it catching rain or snow runoff from the roof. If you live in a freeze-thaw climate you may need to deal with heave in the future, so be sure to dig footings below the frost line. Carpet is always a "no" on ramps.

## Parking

Aim for perfection for your parking spot – just enough slope/cross slope for water to drain away (2%) and not take your wheels out of your reach. It's devastating when you pull your chair from your car only to have it roll away... Give yourself transfer space plus room to maneuver around your car door while it's open.

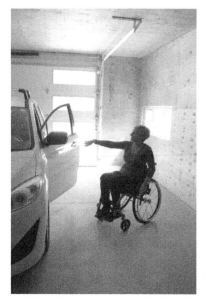

Okay, yes, we staged this photo quite a bit – who has a garage this clean? Well, not us! The point is though, that you need to have lots of space to get in and out of your vehicle, especially if you have a side-access van.

I've been told that there is no such thing as a "too big" garage. Give yourself enough space to park all your wheels, not just your car. You may have a bike (trike) or maybe even a motorcycle! You never know – so go as big as you can afford. If you think you might one day own a truck, you should consider the height of the ceiling in your garage. There are many wheelchair lift & load mechanisms that require height, so plan for space above your vehicle, not just around it. Be sure to include an automatic garage door opener in your budget.

Just as with ramps, you need to consider slope. Plan for transfer space and room to get around your car, including removing things from the trunk. Keep in mind that you may not always have the same size car as you do now.

### Wheel-wash station

If you live where winter happens, on a gravel road or you roll through a parking lot (ever), you'll want to have a space to wash your wheels. Don't use your shower! Set up a space that is just larger than your turning radius, add a drain and a small length of hose.  Add a small scrub brush for the really muddy days and a low pile mat to roll dry on and then you can "wipe your feet" before you go in the house. If a full wash station is not an option, hang a scrub brush made with stiff nylon in an easy-to-access location so you can leave the dirt behind.

## Mudroom

It's tough to maneuver around shoes and boots left on the entry floor. A mudroom can help alleviate that problem, but you have to plan your space carefully. Boots and shoes need to be kicked off to one side so you can roll through the other. Coats and backpacks can hang out of the way with easy pull-out drawers or small bins for hats and mitts. On "your" side, have a mat to wipe your wheels on and in the middle, you have (the potential for) a clear path of travel. Your family many need some training – my kids often found their boots and shoes thrown out on the driveway when they left them in my way. A hard lesson to learn when it's raining!

## Exercise space

You are going to be happier and live longer when you exercise, so allow room for it in your design. You may need space for a standing frame or a rowing machine. Remember to account for transfer space if you use a wheelchair. Plan to attach things (like stretchy bands) to the walls – so add extra backing (¾" plywood) to those areas. Proper storage for hand weights will give you space to keep them safely out of the way. Add a mirror if you can, as it will help you check your posture (and the size of your muscles).

## Laundry room

If you are lucky enough to have a whole room for laundry, then the style of doors you choose is not really an issue. But, if your laundry is in a closet or another tucked-away space, choose

83

doors that work best for you. Swing-open doors mean you have to get around them; the same goes for bifold doors. Sliding or pocket doors require less maneuvering, but you have to have the strength to move them. Try for sliding doors that disappear into a pocket and are out of the way altogether.

Stacking your washer and dryer is the ultimate in space efficiency, but if you are in a seated position that's not really an option. What is necessary is a front load washer. How you set up your machines is a personal preference. Using a pedestal or raised platform allows you to reach into the machines without having to lean too far forward. The additional height of a pedestal may prevent you from using the surface of the machine for storage.

Make sure the controls are on the front of each machine. Dials that are easy to turn and buttons that are large and can be pushed by a closed fist (rather than just one finger) are necessary for those with limited dexterity. Door swing is also important. If your washer is on the left (because of the location of the plumbing) make sure the door opens to the left and the dryer door opens to the right. It's very frustrating to have to navigate around the doors with a full load of wet laundry. Visit your local big box store to try out different set-ups and machines. Open the doors and see if you can reach the back to get that one sock that is always stuck there...

Drying for free on your own clothesline is really the ultimate in laundry satisfaction. Set up your laundry in a location near your exterior door. Install a line that raises and lowers and a platform for your laundry basket. You can use the top of your machines for "lay flat to dry" and install a rod for "hang to dry" items above or beside your machine.

For twenty years I have lived without a laundry sink and now I finally have one! You don't have to have a standard white plastic tub with ugly taps. But it can be. Choose a tub with a shallow basin so it will be easier to fill a bucket and get it over the edge of the sink (or just put less water in it). Lever taps are easiest to operate when you have mucky hands. Store your laundry products on low shelving because soap bottles tend to be heavy. Single-use cleaning pods are easy to manage if you have the dexterity to do so.

Your cleaning products also need to be within reach. You never know when your cat will barf on the floor and you are the only one home to clean it up. Keep a kitchen scraper in your cleaning supplies bin; this makes it easier to clean up spills from a seated position. Have a big bin of rags handy for mopping up wet tires or wiping them down before you track snow melt everywhere.

Make space in your laundry room, mudroom or in a closet to hang your lightweight vacuum on the wall. Doing so means you can reach it knowing it's always charged and ready to go. Leaning it in a corner (or in the back of the closet) makes it susceptible to falling over and becoming out of reach.

## Entertainment & Activity

*Living & dining room*

Design your entertainment space with the end in mind; what is it that you like to do? If you like to get together with friends, your house will be the "go to" space! You will be able to spend more time with your friends and family and it will reduce the stress caused by trying to get into a non-accessible space.

Plan your living room as a space to relax and watch TV. You'll need to have furniture that is easy to transfer to and clear space for your mobility device. You can also provide a space where, if you are a wheelchair user, you can roll up and park beside other furniture. If you have space for a coffee table or footrest, make sure it is lightweight and easy to push around.

*COUCH ACCESS*
*We have always had "hand-me-down"*
*couches in our living room. The ones we had*
*(up until very recently) were too soft and low*
*for me to get out of on my own. I needed a*
*lift from Theo in order to get back into my*

*chair. One thing about using a wheelchair is it always keeps you separated from others, even if you pull up right beside them. Not being able to get on and off the couch myself made it impossible for me to sit with my family – I really missed that feeling of being together. I'm a "physical touch" kind of person; I need to be close. After we moved into the new house, I bought a sofa set that I could transfer to and from independently. Snuggling on the couch with my family – you cannot put a price tag on that!*

Your dining room requires more than just space for a table. You'll need space under the table (for knee clearance) and on one or more sides for a mobility device to get around. Proximity of the kitchen to the dining room is an obvious thing to think about. Remember to put your dishes and cutlery on the dining room side of the kitchen.

## Play and workspace

Although I would normally say that "carpet sucks", the playroom may be a place to have a carpet. A small, low pile area rug will help designate the play space, where the toys should be. Then you can have a clear space around the area rug for travel. Create low shelving with lots of accessible storage in clearly labeled plastic bins to help keep the space fun for everyone. Rotate toys to an out-of-sight place and purge regularly to keep things in the playroom manageable.

It's tricky to have enough room for everything in an office and still keep it accessible. You'll need room for your computer, printer, files, work surface, books, etc. As you plan your workspace (at home or at the office), don't just think about knee clearance; plan for enough room to move from side to side without running into table legs. You need to be able to reach for books, printouts, controls, etc. without having to move out and around your table supports.

Bookshelves can be as tall as you like; just keep the books you like where you can reach them. Heavy/awkward books should be placed on the lower shelves. For hobbies, you'll need a large worktable with proper knee clearance and easy-to-reach storage space. Storage bins made from fabric that are small to medium in size are best as they don't get over filled and become too heavy to manage. Label the bins according to the projects you are working on; that way if you need your work surface for something else (like dinner) you can sweep the project into the bin for another day.

# Industry Expert: Creating an inclusive landscape

This next section gives you perspectives from Paul VanderMolen of LawnMaster in Seaforth. He and his team of summer-loving people worked incredibly hard to create an inclusive landscape for me and my family. I interviewed Paul while he was in the "grass seed" stage of the project. Here is what he had to say:

*How has working on the Sawchuk project been different than other landscapes you have created in the past?*

The Sawchuk plan was all about overcoming challenges. There are always challenges when planning a landscape, and not just at a new construction, but what Julie and her family needed put me back into learning mode. Working on the Sawchuk plan was not just about how to make the landscape fit with the design of the home, it was about making it as functional as possible. Every part of the project had to be practical, low effort, include safety, sightlines and, of course, beauty.

*How did you get started with this project?*

I was involved right from the home design phase. Julie and Theo shared their first plan with me, so I had time to think about and research different design aspects. I also spent time with Julie, talking about what she wanted to be able to do outside of her house. I learned from her how everything she does "costs energy" and I realized that the landscape plans needed to be able to reduce that personal energy expenditure. Things like having thresholds as level as possible, choosing a surface that had less friction and smaller, more level joints were all important.

*What does an accessible landscape look like?*

I have learned that making outdoor spaces *accessible* is not enough! We also need to make them *inclusive*. It's one thing for a person to be able to get out on a patio to be outside. It's a whole different matter when that person can maneuver safely onto the grass to lie in the sun or play with their kids or their dog.

Another example of inclusion is being able to independently wheel through a garden to pick some flowers, weed or plant vegetables. Rolling on a lawn can be difficult, so we are creating a yard that is going to be as smooth and level as possible.

I have also changed how we think about sight lines. We were going to plant some tall grasses out front, but as I thought about it and spent more time with Julie, I realized that the grasses I had planned would be too tall for her to see over.

What I understand now is that inclusion means not just access but incorporating all the senses possible. Visually pleasing plantings and stones, smooth surfaces that are within reach (to put your tea on).    Plantings must produce habitat for birds and insects; flowers and plants should have scent and be edible – everything matters! We will also be building raised beds so Julie can wheel along at a height that allows her to reach across to weed, plant and harvest vegetables.

*Was there anything really new that you had to consider? Or anything that was particularly challenging?*

Something new for me was learning about core body temperature. I had no idea how a spinal cord injury affected temperature regulation and it made me understand the need for shade and staying cool. We'll be putting up a pergola and planting trees for shade.

There were also some places where, for safety reasons, we wanted to limit access, so wheels would not roll off the edge of the stone.

Another challenge was managing other people's expectations and understandings. Team work is key for all the parties doing the work, from the surveyors, to heavy equipment operators, dump truck drivers and those laying the stone – we all had to understand how to keep it inclusive with respect to the pathways for walking, the parking of cars, sightlines and garden wall height. Every little decision makes a big difference – we almost built the wall one brick taller than we needed it to be, which would have affected Julie's ability to transfer off the top surface.

*What advice can you offer about choosing a landscape company?*

I'm sure that Julie has talked about this a lot already, but communication is key. Spending time with Julie and really understanding how to help her reduce personal energy expenditure was important. I'm not afraid to speak candidly and ask questions that help me understand her point of view. I've said, "What are the rules?" to find out as much as I can about what it's like to live with a disability.

When you are choosing someone to build YOUR outdoor space, make sure it is someone you can be comfortable sharing your life with. They also need to accept responsibility and be passionate about the whole project, not just the landscape. My team had to consider transitions from one space to another, like at the door thresholds, parking spaces and the driveway. We had to learn more and go above and beyond what we have done in the past. The team you choose must be willing to do that, too.

### Chapter 5: Summary

- ❏ Bathroom – bathing, sink, toilet, grab bars and storage
- ❏ Kitchen – counters, sinks, appliances, storage
- ❏ Bedroom – bed, closet, kids' rooms
- ❏ Access etc. – ramps, parking, mudroom, laundry, exercise space
- ❏ Entertainment space – not just the couch; have room for games and books too

❑ Outdoors – create some space outside: flat, shaded and green

# Alternative ways to live with access

*BUILD YOUR SPACE* was written not just about building a brand-new home. It was written so you could choose information about whatever space you need to change. It might be your workshop, bathroom or garage. The info on how to do that is here. It's the space that YOU need to change for what is best for YOUR needs. This chapter tells stories about different people I have met who have built for access, but not in the traditional way. Or, like Lorie, did it a long time ago, and it is still working for them.

## Renovating the old to *make do*

If renovation is the way you are going to accommodate your needs – it is possible! You can still get what you need; it is just going to require a bit of creativity. Use all the details provided in this book, make the plans, talk to your people and make it happen!

Perhaps I should have written about this first, because we renovated before we built! We did what we needed in order for me to come home from the rehab hospital. We were living in a 110-year-old farmhouse on ten acres. It was an old farmhouse that had addition on addition on addition, so that eventually the original farmhouse could only be seen from the inside. Each one of those add-ons was on a slightly different level. Not only did we have to build a ramp to get into the house, we needed threshold ramps to accommodate all of those level changes. The ramp to the house was built at a 1:12 slope with a railing along the length and a set of stairs at the other end. A cement pad was poured at the bottom of the ramp along with a short section of sidewalk. This allowed a flat, relatively gravel-free surface to park the car alongside.

The bathroom needed the most modification. The vanity came out and a wall-hung sink with a few inches of counter on either side went in. The bathtub came out and a roll-in shower unit went in. It was a tight space for me to access because a window prevented the shower from being any larger. It had a rubber lip that was supposed to prevent water from escaping, but that broke down over time due to wear and tear. A new hand-held shower wand was put in on a rod so it could slide up and down.

No changes were made to the toilet until after I had been home for several months, until I gained strength and "bathroom skills". Eventually, a tall toilet with an oval bowl and a front-open seat was installed with grab bars on either side. Changes were also made to accommodate storage for supplies and towels and to the height of the mirror over the sink. The light switch was moved during the renovation in order for me to reach it.

In the kitchen we made only a few changes. The cupboard under the sink was removed and backing was installed to hide the plumbing. Two lower cupboards were removed, and drawers were made to store dishes and pots so I could reach them.

For our "new" main floor bedroom, we moved the piano to act as a screen and put some curtains on the glass doors. Originally, we were going to widen several doorways inside the house, but in the end, we decided that it was going to be too costly (and messy) to do. Only one door needed to be replaced and that was in the main entry; it became a 36" door.

## Condo living

When Jenna decided it was time for her to spread her wings and leave her parents' home, the move did not happen quickly. Jenna uses a manual wheelchair to assist with her mobility; she was born with spina bifida. Finding a wheelchair-accessible apartment or condominium in Vancouver was next to impossible. There were so many limitations – not just steps, but very narrow doorways, tiny kitchens and carpet impossible to roll on.

In Jenna's kitchen you'll find a roll-under workspace and pull-down cupboards. This makes for much more efficient use of space in her condo kitchen.

Initially, the idea of making an "accessible condo" was a bit off-putting for Jenna. She was uncomfortable with the idea that her home may end up highlighting her limitations to her friends and family. Jenna found a team of people to design and renovate her condo who admitted that UD was generally new to them. "It was important that they were willing to be vulnerable about what UD means and were willing to learn how to do it effectively." Together they developed a true understanding of the concepts and benefits of Universal Design. Doing so allowed Jenna to realize that her UD home would allow her to be safer, independent, dignified, capable and able to thrive – a true representation of her as a person.

Cooking from a seated position meant that Jenna's kitchen needed to have a lowered cooking surface, a side-swing wall oven at chest height, lowered counters with knee clearance and cupboards with drop-down shelving. In previous kitchens, she was only ever able to reach the first shelf, leaving everything to be "organized" on the counter instead. Jenna's friends love the shelves that lower too – they are not just designed for those who use a wheelchair. The most exciting part of her new kitchen is the oven at chest height, allowing her to be more creative than macaroni and cheese. Jenna says, "Now I get to learn how to cook like Jamie Oliver and Gordon Ramsay!"

In her bedroom closet, Jenna removed the shelving and replaced it with bars that can be pulled down. Doing this meant she could hang everything up and no longer needed her dresser, giving her more space to maneuver and maximize storage space. Jenna's favourite part of the bathroom remodel is the recessed cabinets under the counter that allow her to roll under, face the mirror and get ready for her day. It's the perfect location for make-up application – and much more convenient than using the kitchen table.

Another unique part of the UD in Jenna's condo is the "flex room". This space is part pantry, part office, part closet. The versatility of the design gives some counter space, drop-down shelves and additional storage for things that are not used often.

One aspect that Jenna didn't have to change were the doorways – they were built wide and with pocket doors. Pocket doors are the most efficient use of space for cramped quarters, especially in bathrooms where turning radius is paramount.

Jenna has not been shy about sharing her renovation story. It's her hope that others will learn about the benefits of building with UD and that the costs associated with it will go down as more people use it. "It broke my heart to see the quotes [for this project] and know that others would not be able to afford to do it."

What is Jenna's advice to anyone planning to build or renovate? She recommends that you have an open and honest conversation with those who are doing the work. She says, "Remember, there is no one-size-fits-all solution for accessibility. Put yourself in the best possible position to grow and learn and have the confidence to ask the right questions."

## A home away from home

This is Craig. He's a farmer in Saskatchewan who spends his winters in Texas. Early on, after the accident that caused his spinal cord injury, Craig realized that travelling with a wheelchair and relying on hotels to be accessible for his needs was not the way

to go. He decided that he'd be better off travelling with his own home.

This queen size bed is in the back of the bus. The photographer is standing in the bathroom which leads to the kitchen and then the front section of the bus with the table and chairs.

This motorcoach (which to me looks like a bus for some wicked rock band) has everything Craig and his wife need. With a queen size bed in the back, bathroom with sliding door and hand controls added on, it is wide enough to accommodate his wheelchair through the aisles and gives him several places to turn around. Craig says, "Floorplan is key". The coach can actually sleep four people when the couch is folded down.

Kitchen appliances are all within reach from a side approach. The bathroom is "galley style" but has everything needed, including a bathtub. With his T12 injury he has the strength and balance to transfer into the small tub; similar to what he does at home. However, Craig says it may not work for someone who relies on different aids to use the toilet and shower.

For Craig, getting in and out of the coach was the only major challenge to making it work. With a unique side entry, just wide enough to accommodate his chair, Craig mounted a Superarm lift. The lift and the addition of hand controls for driving were the only modifications he made to the motorcoach.

The lift is called a Superarm Basement Lift built by Handicaps Inc in Englewood, Colorado. It is called a basement lift because in addition to the swingarm that lifts you up into the coach, it also raises an additional two feet prior to the swing to accommodate for the additional height. The rider is suspended by straps to the wheelchair, different than a platform lift which takes up more space. For Craig, this is a big advantage because he is able to spin his wheels to clean them while suspended.

The coach is 45 ft long, 8½ feet wide and when he tows his van, he has almost 70 feet in total length. Craig even has a storage space below the coach for traveling with his Omeo! His former experience as a long-haul trucker makes him comfortable maneuvering such a vehicle.

Craig's advice about buying an accessible coach or motorhome? "Do your homework. Slideouts make a unit virtually inaccessible when the slides are in." He also wants readers to keep in mind that it needs to be stored when not in use, which has its costs as well. "If it's in use full time then that is not an issue but camping fees can add up; Walmart camping is only a short-term solution."

Final Thoughts: Be creative. A wooden spoon will get a cup on the top shelf down just as well as a fancy reacher will. If your chair rolls away from you in the tub, a wet towel rolled up will bring it back if you throw it just right, and quicker than waiting for someone to come bail you out. Sometimes it's just easier to find ways to adapt to the world vs expecting the world to adapt to us.

## Designing for aging in place

Lorie's life changed when a serious fall down the basement stairs left her with a skull fracture and impaired mobility. Three years earlier, in 1998, she had been diagnosed with Multiple Sclerosis (MS), but up until her fall she had not given much thought to accessibility in her own home. She already lived in a bungalow but didn't realize until she moved into her new home how much of a difference it would make.

When Lorie and her husband Kevin built in 2001, it was at a time when most contractors were not aware of the need for looking to the future and building to "age in place". MS is an unpredictable, untreatable disease – so Lorie and Kevin planned a home that had the accessibility she needed now and considered the possible future use of a wheelchair. Even without such a diagnosis, Lorie wants to encourage everyone building a home to take a look at what their needs will be as they age.

The home is built on a cement pad, with heated floors and no stairs. Lorie wanted beautiful vaulted ceilings, but Kevin thought it best to keep the roofline low to allow for easy upkeep. The windows are floor to ceiling, which gives a lot of natural light and excellent visibility. One section of the kitchen counter is lowered; currently it is used as a computer desk but in the future, it could become a seated prep counter. They have a wall oven and a second sink beside the stove for pouring pot water. From island to counter the space is wide enough for two people as well as an assistive device.

All doors (36") and halls (5') are wide, which Lorie thinks is a good practice for any build because it makes moving furniture so much easier! The flooring is the same throughout the house to prevent trip hazards. They left light switches at standard height; however, Lorie wished she had known to lower the one beside the bed so she could reach it lying down. The "kids" bathroom is not fully accessible, but still large enough to get her walker in. The master bathroom has a roll-in shower.

Although this looks like a small office space, it is in Lorie's kitchen. She designed it for the future for the if/when situation of requiring the use of a wheelchair. It will then become the prep-counter that she'll use while seated.

Kevin and Lorie built all of these features into a home that looks just like, in their words, a "standard home" that works for now and will also in the future. Lorie is able to drive her scooter through the doors and right to the pantry and the fridge. Independent grocery shopping would otherwise be impossible. Her scooter is a very important part of life – not just for shopping but for a change of view in a roll around town. She parks it in the laundry room for charging.

After 18 years of living there, there are not too many things they would change. But one would be the wooden deck in the back of the house (go with cement, less maintenance) and the other would be to do a level, "not gravel" surface at the front to park on. The driveway surface is usually the last part to happen in a new build; most people are out of money by then, too!

As was mentioned at the start of Lorie's story, her new home changed her life. She had not realized how much of her available energy was being used up by everyday tasks like bathing and household chores. With her home set up for her needs, she had energy left for family, friends and living life. When asked if her house "fits" with the others on her street Lorie said: "None of the design changes [we made] compromised the style or feel of our home but they made immeasurable improvements to my life every day. The accessibility of our home is a feature that we are proud of and often show off when people come to visit."

## Wheel Pad - A place to go home to

This is a fantastic idea that I wish had been around at the time of my accident. It's called "Wheel Pad" and it's based on the idea of a Tiny Home. As you likely already know, finding or renovating a house to be ready in time for someone to come home to after rehab is a huge challenge. Wheel Pad is an entire suite (bedroom, bathroom and living space) that can be added on to an existing home.

Wheel Pad is designed to be added on to an existing home. It contains a washroom and bedroom, both completely accessible. Two doors give access; one to the outdoors and one that attaches to the home's existing door or window.

The idea came from Architect Joseph Cincotta and Julie Lineberger of LineSync Architecture in Wilmington, Vermont. Their nephew Riley Poor sustained an SCI at age 26 and had to stay in a hotel after rehab – there was nowhere accessible for him to go. Julie and Joseph realized that there was a need for a modular design to help newly-injured people have a place for support and recovery near their families.

Wheel Pad ramps up to an exterior door and then a second entry that is attached to a door or window of an existing home. The ramp to the exterior door accommodates the change in level and allows the person in need to have privacy and independence. The whole unit can be brought and attached to a home, and then removed when/if no longer needed.

Inside, the bedroom and bathroom have high ceilings and large windows to make the space feel roomy. A lift track is embedded in the ceiling to take the occupant from the bedroom directly into the bathroom. The roll-in shower has a sloped floor in a space that is designed to be a "wet room". Construction materials are lightweight and durable (and environmentally friendly) and furnishings are left to be chosen by the new owner.

Using Wheel Pad attached to the family home means people can have privacy when needed and yet they access the main living area of the home. When support workers or friends come, they can access the accommodations through the separate entrance. The overall size is 220' square, but it can be customized. There is an XL version that also contains a larger living space.

Riley now lives in his own accessible home designed by LineSync Architecture and constructed by Riley's Dad. He and his girlfriend Andrea are currently designing and building their own accessible motor home that they are taking on tour across the United States to share what they have learned about UD and building for access.

## A house for Luke and Zane

When Debbie and her husband planned their new house, they made decisions that would be helpful for their teenage sons Lucas and Zane to be as independent as possible. They have a very rare disease called Morquio Syndrome. The disease affects many parts of their bodies, leading them to have very short stature. They also have very loose joints which causes a significant decrease in grip strength. Sadly, they lost their son Lucas as a result of a complication from a major surgery. This happened during the build.

Both the teenage boys were approximately three feet tall, so they built doorways with zero thresholds. At some point in the boys' lives they could require electric wheelchairs as their mobility (walking and doing stairs) was already restricted. At the time of the build both boys were mobile, so their height was the key thing taken into consideration when they planned the house.

Zane stands in his roll-in shower to show that the grab bars and shower controls are placed low so he can reach them. There is also a towel hook at just the right height.

Some of the features in the home that were designed for the boys include light switches that are lower; the microwave is built into the island down low for them to access. Their bathroom was created specifically for them with a roll-in shower, grab bars down low, a shower chair and a tiny sink. They installed a bidet toilet seat for personal hygiene and independence.

The flooring is vinyl plank glued down to handle wheelchair traffic if necessary, in the future. The door handles are all levers which help the boys open doors with their decreased grip strength. The windows in the home are lower so the boys could see outside.

Before building they had considered moving and renovating, but the cost to renovate (even the simple things) was so expensive it became obvious that building from the ground up made more sense. It cost no more to put the lights switches lower or order the window style that was needed. When making the home zero threshold, the landscaping was done to make it aesthetically pleasing.

Designing the home to be accessible also made it easier for the boys' grandparents to visit. Debbie also said that she and her husband plan to live in the home long enough to personally use and enjoy the accessible aspects of the home as well.

Debbie's front walk shows that a home built with UD in mind does not have to stand out as "different" and that it can be beautiful!

## A Quick Build

Michelle and her husband Daryl quickly built a new house after the car accident that left Michelle with quadriplegia at age 50. The build was designed as a bungalow with a basement and it had to be completed in time for her to go home to when she finished her rehabilitation in hospital.

The tricky thing about a spinal cord injury is that no one knows how much sensory or motor function one will regain – even doctors and rehab therapists are not able to guess what the patient will be capable of, given time. When Michelle was told that she would not have the use of her hands nor the use of her legs, that was what they planned for. She was fitted for a motorized wheelchair (which are much larger and heavier than a manual wheelchair) and was told she would not be able to have the dexterity to cook or do laundry, let alone her own personal care.

After three years of intense physiotherapy and an extreme amount of determination, Michelle has regained some of her hand function and a good deal of strength in her core. She has also learned to propel herself in a manual wheelchair. Now, Michelle wishes they had built the house a bit differently. Originally, they were told to "assume worst case scenario" and build for it, which they did. The house is all one level, with wide doors and a roll-in shower, but with the returned hand function Michelle could have made use of a more functional kitchen.

Michelle and Daryl had not planned for her to make such an awesome recovery. There was no advice that said she would be able to cook and do laundry, so the kitchen has a regular stove and they have a top load washing machine. While the washer may seem like an easy fix (just switch out for a front load) changing to a different cooking layout is not. This would involve a roll-under cooktop, a wall mounted oven and more undercounter access for her knees. Making these changes now would require renovating their brand-new kitchen.

It's not just the inside of the house where they could have done things differently, but the outside also. The lot where they built required a fairly steep driveway, and now that Michelle has use of a manual wheelchair, she wishes that it were not that way. She has some grip and strength with her hands and arms, but not enough to propel her up the steep slope. When she goes out and about in her small town, she uses power assist.

When I interviewed Michelle for this book, she said that although she loves her house, she wishes they had had time before building in order to plan for her to be more independent. Michelle also knows that as she ages her abilities and circumstances may change, so being prepared for that is now her goal.

# If I could, I would...

What would I do differently? Sometimes we have to learn from our mistakes. Here are a few stories from folks who also built for accessibility.

**Michelle**: We bought and renovated a cottage. Once the doors out onto the deck were installed, we realized we should have put in French doors instead of a sliding door. The weight of the door and the track for the sliders interfere with my ability to come and go independently. Also, the bathroom door is not wide enough – I take a chance with my knuckles every day. (SCI; uses a power chair and a manual chair)

**Mark**: When you have a couple of kids and a wife, there ends up being a lot of shoes! If I were to build again, I would create a space that is easy for family members to store their outdoor clothes and shoes so that I don't have to find my way around them or bend over to get them out of the way. (SCI; uses a manual chair)

**Ralph**: I spent most of my time planning to have an accessible space to work in my garage. It worked out really well and I am able to do my hobbies independently. I'm not really a cook, but I wish I had created a space in the kitchen that was "roll under" so that I can be more comfortable when I help with kitchen clean-up. (SCI; uses a manual chair)

**Megan**: I love that my house looks like any other house and I can come and go without needing a ramp. I wish I had made my ensuite larger with more room on either side of the toilet and a

lower counter that I can roll under to do my makeup. In the kitchen, I need a bit more space under my sink for my knees and toes so that I can reach the sink properly without straining my shoulders. (SCI; uses a manual chair)

**Charlene**: My biggest wish for my son is for him to have safe access to the outdoors. I would blow out that window, put in a door and build a deck with a screened-in porch. That way he could be outside and protected from the sun and the bugs. (son Dean has a rare genetic disorder and uses a wheelchair)

**Chris**: I wish I had made the guest bathroom more accessible – a bit larger and with a sink that is easier to access. Also, in the kitchen, I would make the upper cabinets "pull down" so I would be able to reach more than just the lowest shelf. (SCI; uses a manual wheelchair)

**Jenna**: I wouldn't do anything differently! We stuck to the timelines, had the perfect design, the perfect team, and everyone was open and communicative. My goal was to figure out how to make it functional and beautiful – and I did! (Spina bifida; manual wheelchair user)

## Chapter 6: Summary

- ❏ Renovation – changing the space you have and making it work
- ❏ Condo – high-rise and accessible
- ❏ Accessible on wheels – travel with your personalized space
- ❏ Aging in Place – 18 years and still working well
- ❏ Wheel Pad – adding to your current space; temporary or not
- ❏ Luke and Zane's house – a special build for the boys
- ❏ A Quick Build – when time is tight
- ❏ Lessons learned from those with experience

# In the end, you'll build it YOUR way

*Build YOUR Space* was written to inspire you to change how you think about creating accessible living spaces. Plan your design, construction, heat source, electrical considerations, windows, outdoor space and even furniture placement; in the end you will have a space that is exactly how YOU need it to be. Start by planning for now and for the future; bring your team in to be a part of that process so they understand the "whys" of your decisions.

Look at your lifestyle and your specific needs for safety, how you can be as independent as possible and what your future self may require. Communicate with those who will help you, so they understand how little decisions are important for your comfort.

Next you need to think about YOUR space room by room. Much will depend on what kind of space you are working with – renovation, new build or addition, but anything is possible when you think outside the traditional four walls.

# Appendix

## Universal Design

The 7 Principles of Universal Design were developed in 1997 by a working group of architects, product designers, engineers and environmental design researchers, led by the late Ronald Mace at North Carolina State University. The purpose of the Principles is to guide the design of environments, products and communications. According to the Center for Universal Design at North Carolina State University, the Principles "may be applied to evaluate existing designs, guide the design process and educate both designers and consumers about the characteristics of more usable products and environments."

*Principle 1: Equitable Use*

The design is useful and marketable to people with diverse abilities.

*Principle 2: Flexibility in Use*

The design accommodates a wide range of individual preferences and abilities.

*Principle 3: Simple and Intuitive Use*

Use of the design is easy to understand, regardless of the user's experience, knowledge, language skills, or current concentration level.

*Principle 4: Perceptible Information*

The design communicates necessary information effectively to the user, regardless of ambient conditions or the user's sensory abilities.

*Principle 5: Tolerance for Error*

The design minimizes hazards and the adverse consequences of accidental or unintended actions.

*Principle 6: Low Physical Effort*

The design can be used efficiently and comfortably and with a minimum of fatigue.

*Principle 7: Size and Space for Approach and Use*

Appropriate size and space is provided for approach, reach, manipulation, and use regardless of user's body size, posture, or mobility.

From the Centre for Excellence in Universal Design, Dublin, Ireland
http://universaldesign.ie/What-is-Universal-Design/The-7-Principles

# Glossary

**Drop Zone** – this is a fancy term for a place where you frequently place items temporarily. Usually it is a countertop beside the fridge or microwave; it could also be a pull-out counter in either of those spaces or below/beside the oven. Making it heat-proof is a good idea.

**Lap board** – really, it's just a cutting board that I use to carry things on my lap – sometimes even a cat! Mine has a ridge around the inside edge to hold spills (like coffee) so they don't land in my lap.

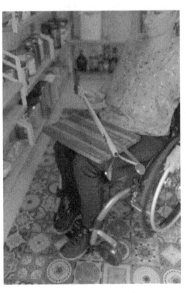

**Reacher** – a tool with a long handle and pinchers (or suction cups) that allows items to be picked up off the floor or reached from a height. It is often used by people who cannot safely bend to the floor or who are in a seated position and cannot reach items on shelves.

**Sliderboard** – a wooden board with a smooth, shellacked surface used to help a person transfer from one seated position to another. One side of the board is placed under the hip and the person just slides across to the other surface; for example, from wheelchair to bed.

**Spinal Cord Injury** – this type of injury is usually traumatic, caused by a car accident or fall from a height. A region of the spinal cord is damaged, either in part or completely, resulting in some type of paralysis (paraplegia or quadriplegia). The damage to the spinal cord is not reversible and requires the injured to use some type of mobility device, often a wheelchair. Injuries most often are permanent.

**Transfer** – people without the use of their legs need to move from one seated position to another without standing. This is referred to as a transfer. Examples include moving from wheelchair to seat in a car or from wheelchair to shower bench. The first rule in planning transfers is safety. It is also important to have enough space for a wheelchair to maneuver up to and beside the seat the person is moving to. This picture shows me doing a transfer using a sliderboard from my chair to my bed.

**Universal Design** – describes the concept of designing all products and the built environment to be aesthetic and usable to the greatest extent possible by everyone, regardless of their age, ability, or status in life. See Appendix for more details.

**Zero Threshold** – a design feature for entryways, or where there is a change in flooring, that allows for there to be a minimal amount of level change. This prevents trip hazards and allows mobility devices to pass over the threshold smoothly. This idea is typically applied to exterior doors and roll-in showers.

# Resources

The following is a list of resources that you may find useful for additional information and for digging deeper.

Accessibility for Ontarians with Disabilities Act

https://www.aoda.ca/

Centre for Excellence in Universal Design

http://universaldesign.ie/What-is-Universal-Design/

Grab Bars Canada

https://www.grabbarscanada.com/

The Rick Hansen Foundation

https://www.rickhansen.com/become-accessible/accessibility-resources

Universal Design Tool Kit

https://www.universaldesigntoolkit.com

# Julie can help YOU

**Do you need help creating an accessible space? Ask Julie.**
As well as creating her own showcase home, Julie has helped local businesses, big and small, build for access. From the ground up, back to the bricks or just a few tweaks, get the help you need to do it right, and not break the bank.
*Clients include*:
Toyota Canada, LUX Hotel (Blyth), Blyth Cowbell Brewing Co., DEAMS property management, GJAJ Holdings (Rutledge Development, Blyth)

**Would you like a dynamic speaker at your next event or staff training day? Invite Julie.**
As a trained teacher and professional speaker, Julie knows what makes people listen – real stories.
*Julie has been a guest of:*
University of Western Ontario: School of Nursing & Ivey School of Business Leaders Forum, University of Guelph Accessibility Conference 2019, Community Living, North Perth Community of Character, Ontario Optimists, Women's Institute, Ontario Bike Summit, Elementary and High Schools across Southwestern Ontario

**Would you like your business to be Rick Hansen Foundation Certified Accessible? Julie can do that, too.**
The RHFAC certification program will help you showcase the work you have done to make your space accessible. Julie will help you through the process and will complete the rating survey and report. The RHFAC is the only accessibility rating recognized by the Canadian Standards Association.
*Businesses certified by Julie include:*
Blyth Cowbell Brewing Co. – RHFAC Gold (Brewery and Restaurant), and other Ontario projects are currently top secret!

# About the Author

Julie Sawchuk is an accessibility expert in Ontario. Since the accident in 2015 that caused her spinal cord injury, she has been sharing what she has experienced through her writing and speaking. Using her personal experience and professional training, she helps businesses improve access to and within their buildings, from the ground up.

Julie's projects include two international airports, Blyth Cowbell Brewing Co., and Rutledge Property Development. In 2018, she and her husband Theo built a completely wheelchair-accessible home on their ten-acre farm outside of Blyth.

Julie is a Rick Hansen Foundation Ambassador and RHFAC® Accessibility Strategist. She is a professional speaker who shares her message about accessibility and inclusion with students, all types of businesses as well as municipal and provincial governments.

While Julie's first career was as a teacher, she is now a published author from the best-selling book *Shine 3: Inspirational Stories of Overcoming Adversity.* She writes a monthly column about accessibility for North Huron Publishing's *The Citizen* and the blog "Living with Paralysis".

*Build YOUR Space* showcases Julie's new home, highlighting all the tips and tricks that help save personal energy, improve safety, increase independence and preserve dignity.

Invite Julie to speak at your school, your next event or use her professional services to improve the accessibility of YOUR built environment.

You can find Julie at the following:

e-mail julie@juliesawchuk.ca

website juliesawchuk.ca

@sawesome_julie on Instagram

@JulieSawesome on Twitter

and as Julie Sawchuk on YouTube

8 8 0
1 2 / 4 0
1 6 0 / 4 0
8 2 / 8 4 0
9 1

Made in the USA
Monee, IL
06 January 2021